ISRAELI
BUSINESS CULTURE

Building Effective Business
Relationships with Israelis

Osnat Lautman

Revised and Expanded Second Edition

ISRAELI BUSINESS CULTURE
Building Effective Business Relationships with Israelis
Revised and Expanded Second Edition

The seven letters of the word "ISRAELI" are used by the author to elaborate on the main characteristics of Israeli business culture. ISRAELI: Informal, Straightforward, Risk-Taking, Ambitious, Entrepreneurial, Loud, Improvisational (ISRAELI™) is a service mark of Osnat Lautman and OLM Consulting – business consulting services in the field of cross-cultural communications.

ISBN: 978-965-92504-5-5

Read Israeli Business Culture before interacting with new contacts, and return to it whenever necessary for added processing of your cross-cultural experiences.

Author Osnat Lautman uses the word **ISRAELI**™ as an acronym to depict the general profile of Israel's business culture:

- I Informal
- S Straightforward
- R Risk-Taking
- A Ambitious
- E Entrepreneurial
- L Loud
- I Improvisational

In this revised and expanded second edition:

Non-Israelis will learn about the origins of the Israeli culture, its main characteristics and how to bridge the gap when working with Israelis. Israelis will gain more awareness of how they are perceived by their colleagues, supervisors and subordinates around the globe. Both Israelis and non-Israelis will acquire tools to enhance communication, which is the cornerstone of profitable business in our diverse global economy.

Tel Aviv skyline (Photo: liorpt, n.d.)

Sponsored by

Contents

Foreword to the Revised and Expanded Second Edition

In September 2015, the first edition of Israeli Business Culture was published. Ninety-five pages of practicality and professionalism, with explanations, anecdotes and recommendations on how to work most optimally with Israelis. The idea was to put out a short, effective handbook of sorts that businesspeople could easily finish reading on a flight. Non-Israelis could learn about the main characteristics of the Israeli culture and how to bridge the gap when working with Israelis, and Israelis could gain a sense of how they are perceived by people from other cultures.

The book quickly became an Amazon bestseller and is also available in select bookstores in Israel. Many readers contacted me with feedback and perceptions from the first edition. Some even posed important additional questions, such as the impact of Israel's history on the nation's business behavior, how to build trust and smooth working relationships with Israelis, and many others.

Such questions by readers, as well as my ever-increasing work with multinational companies, brought me to a deeper, more professional and better-focused understanding of how to address even more of what you should know about Israel. The book has been revised in many ways, with plenty of additional information throughout. This expanded second edition also allows you to choose whether you want further details and insights in what I call "A Closer Look" at the end of most sections of the book.

The book is divided into three main parts:
Israeli Business Culture Background
ISRAELI™ Business Culture Characteristics
The Interplay of ISRAELI™ Characteristics

Israeli Business Culture Background
Learning about any culture needs to start with understanding its roots. This chapter covers Israel's history, borders, defense forces, religion, language, etc., all of which are an inseparable part of who Israelis are in the 21st century. The country's special circumstances and past experiences all impact today's behavior, successes and failures in daily life and business.

ISRAELI™ Business Culture Characteristics
The majority of a country's population tends to conduct itself in a similar manner, with the same behavior patterns and cultural assumptions. In this chapter I present each of the major Israeli characteristics in detail, accompanied by real-life examples and advice for the ideal approach when coming into contact with Israelis. At the end of this chapter, a handy quick-reference section summarizes the ISRAELI™ model and gives concise recommendations.

The Interplay of ISRAELI™ Characteristics
Understanding your colleagues, supervisors and subordinates around the globe is essential for international business success.

This chapter discusses integrative tools that can assist managers, coworkers, vendors, clients and associates in improving communication and maximizing their work with Israelis, and probably with people from other cultures as well.

This book is meant to be helpful and practical. Read it before interacting with new contacts, and return to it whenever necessary for added processing of your cross-cultural experiences.

I have no doubt that both you and your future business partners will benefit.

I hope you enjoy this new edition and that it will bring you special understanding and improved cultural intelligence for working with Israelis in particular and dealing with different cultures in general.

Acknowledgements

I had the privilege of living in the United States with my family for a few years. That period forced me to exit my comfort zone and part from everything that had been familiar to me: my language, culture, friends and extended family. I wish to thank everyone I met during that time in the U.S. for helping me understand the environment I had come from and identify the characteristics of Israeli culture.

Perceiving the deep cultural gap between my former and new homes pushed me to explore the subject further. I conducted countless interviews with businesspeople from all over the world. The list is too long to mention each by name, but I am indebted to them all for sharing with me their experiences of working with Israelis, and thus contributing to the knowledge that went into this book.

Furthermore, I owe significant thanks to all the global companies to whom I provide consulting, workshops and lectures. In each such professional collaboration I always learn more from my clients. Their conversations about the global mindset and their own country's business cultures and values help me crystallize my thoughts and understanding of the nuances of my own culture. I am also very grateful to all the first edition readers who sent me their own examples and insights. Thank you so much for your responses, which allowed me to better understand which ideas warranted a closer look in this second edition.

Deep appreciation goes to Margo Eyon for translating and editing the entire book – both times, and faithfully advising and assisting me through to its completion. Margo, the final product wouldn't have been the same without you. Thank you.

And finally I would like to acknowledge my husband Eli Mansoor, with special thanks for his love and support throughout the writing of this book, as well as his suggestions for improvement and invaluable practical insights drawn from his own business experience. Eli is an inseparable part of my personal and professional life.

With love,
Osnat Lautman

About the Author

Osnat Lautman

- M.A. in Social Science and Communications, Bar Ilan University, Israel

- Certificate in Organizational Development, New York University, New York

Osnat Lautman is a well-known Israeli organizational consultant and the founder of OLM Consulting. She created the ISRAELI™ model of Israeli business characteristics and is an accomplished researcher, author and lecturer. She leads custom-built workshops for a wide variety of Israeli and international clients.

Osnat has extensive global experience in advising CEOs, VPs and employees in multinational organizations. Her customers include: Manufacturers' Association of Israel, Jewish Agency, Verint, NYU Tel Aviv, FIDF, Israel Defense Ministry delegation in New York, JCC Association, NAB, Hebrew University of Jerusalem, 888 Holdings, Corning, SkyVision, ObserveIT, MX1, Rackspace, Israel Export Institute, StartApp, Tel Aviv Municipality, and many others.

Osnat lived in Hoboken, New Jersey, from 2009 to 2013. During this time, she started her extensive research on the differences between Israeli and non-Israeli business cultures, including video interviews with businesspeople from numerous origins. The recorded discussions are incorporated into her lectures and workshops for demonstration purposes.

You may contact Osnat at osnat@olm-consulting.com.

Introduction

Much has been written about the State of Israel, its historical roots, geographical boundaries, local customs, politics, religion, military and defense policy, and outstanding technological achievements. Yet little has been written about its business culture. Despite the vast numbers of Israeli companies that conduct business with international companies, so far no book has explained the Israeli business culture and how to effectively bridge the gaps in mentality and communication between it and the rest of the world. As an organizational consultant specializing in intercultural communication, I have researched precisely this subject and interviewed people from a variety of cultures who shared with me their experiences working with Israelis.

Quora is a website where questions are asked and answered by its community of users. A man who works in Silicon Valley asked, "Why are Israeli people so hard to work with? I know three or four Israelis. One is super smart, the other two are super good marketers, but they are all really, really difficult to work with. Why? Have others had the same experience with Israelis? Why is it so difficult to work with them?" (Quora, 2012). I believe that, after reading this book, businesspeople will no longer feel the same way as the man who expressed all that frustration online. Cultural understanding improves intercultural communication, and fosters genuine, trustworthy business relations.

In my research I have heard claims time and again that Israelis are smart and entrepreneurial in nature, stubbornly persistent, don't practice long-term planning and always think outside the box. Some of these characteristics tend to be valued in the international marketplace. However, in the next breath the interviewees usually mention a variety of difficulties associated with doing business with Israelis. In most cultures Israelis are often perceived as arrogant, aggressive, rude and impulsive.

From the outset of this book, I must emphasize that research on "cultures" deals with groups and therefore leans towards generalizations. Obviously, we must not forget that each member of a group is a unique individual. Many forces combine to make an individual what he is: the home (parents and/or siblings), faith and religion, socioeconomic influences and personal creeds, to name just a few. Every society has members who do not fit the overall cultural mold. In each culture, there will always be those who behave somewhat differently.

What's more, understanding the individual requires first building a pattern so that we can compare it to a general outline, to better comprehend the similarities and differences. In order to see uniqueness—for example in an Israeli who excels in long-term planning, unlike most of her compatriots—you need that base reference of the general cultural pattern. Furthermore, deviations of the minority are not the first thing that meets the eye; on the contrary, the behavior of the majority is noticed before anything else.

A classic step-by-step model by Hoopes (1981, cited in Layes, 2010, p. 113) provides a good example of the way we learn incrementally about another culture:

1. <u>Ethnocentricity</u>: Believing one's own worldview is the only possible one.

2. <u>Awareness of otherness</u>: Recognizing the existence of the other's worldview.

3. <u>Understanding</u>: Honoring the rational of the foreign worldview.

4. <u>Acceptance:</u> Accepting the other's worldview without value judgment.

5. <u>Conscious value judgment</u>: Comparing one's own and the other's worldviews using culturally overlapping, fair standards.

6. <u>Selective adoption</u>: Partially integrating the foreign worldview into one's own worldview.

In other words, based on Hoopes, there are six steps from the time we see only our own culture to when we are able to accept without judgment and even somewhat embrace another culture. In due course we may grasp some subtle differences among subgroups in the same culture; for example, the distinction between East and West Germans; or between not just New Yorkers as opposed to other Americans but even Manhattan residents compared to greater New York area suburbanites or people from other boroughs; or between Jewish French and Christian French, and so forth.

It's very difficult to accurately gauge other cultures if you've never studied or defined your own culture. We use our culture as a compass to relate to and define other cultures in comparison to ourselves. The biggest challenge in working with diverse groups in international companies is not lack of knowledge about the Other, but lack of understanding about Self: our own culture, norms and beliefs, and the powerful, subliminal roots that dictate all of our verbal and nonverbal communication.

Concrete observation of all kinds of behavior does not provide deep cultural understanding of Israel or any other country. If we wish to truly comprehend Israeli business culture, we must look at its sources, values, norms and beliefs. In diverse workshops that I have been leading for many years around the globe, I first divide the participants up according to their countries of origin, e.g., Israelis in one group, Germans in another, Chinese, American, British and so forth. I then ask each group to analyze and list the main values of their culture.

Participants often find this task difficult at first because people don't usually need to assess their own conventions and values in their daily lives. We all tend to just accept social norms at face value, according to how our parents instilled in us the sense of what is and is not acceptable, and the way we see other people around us behaving. Then, in my cross-cultural workshop, they are requested to identify and express their subconscious primary cultural values.

It's quite interesting to see that many Israelis from different companies and professional positions who have participated in my workshops create remarkably similar lists of values. Here are a couple of samples:

ISRAELI VALUES
1. Warm Attitude
2. Family
3. National
4. Brave
5. People Oriented
6. Tradition
7. Creativity
8. Living the moment
9. Straight forward
10. Informal

ISRAELI Values

- Family
- Friendship
- Mutual Responsibility
- To dare
- Military service
- Education
- Risk-taking
- Informal
- Direct
- Criticism

Following is a composite list of the values written in surprisingly almost identical ways by many Israelis who have participated in my workshops over the years:

1. Family oriented

2. National and personal mutual responsibility

3. Directness

4. Warm attitude

5. Risk-taking

6. People oriented

7. Flexibility and creativity

8. Informality

9. Criticism

10. Living in the moment

This is how Israelis list their own values. However, in this book I have chosen to examine in greater depth the way that non-Israelis see Israelis, as well as the roots and underlying values of Israeli behavior.

This book is meant for both Israelis and non-Israelis. Israelis who wish to communicate successfully with people from different cultures will gain insight into their own culture and how their behavior is perceived and interpreted from the outside. Looking at ourselves from other people's perspective is always an effective way to understand our own culture system. This gives Israelis an opportunity to modify their behavior when functioning in diverse groups, to make the communication more productive and pleasing.

Non-Israelis who read this book, on the other hand, will acquire very specific knowledge about the main Israeli culture characteristics, tips for successfully communicating with Israelis, and recommendations on how to behave and make decisions in real-life business situations involving Israelis, all anchored in academic and practical cultural research. Once you know what to expect, working with Israelis becomes a lot easier. You learn to distinguish typical Israeli behavior, to appreciate its origins and advantages, and not to take personally what you may consider negative or abrasive.

The main Israeli business characteristics that I describe in this book derive from dozens of interviews I've conducted with businesspeople who shared their experiences of working with Israelis. I focus on their observations about what is "typically Israeli" in their actual experiences, as well as on my subsequent analyses based on my knowledge and experience in cross-cultural communication. All the non-Israelis, whatever their nationality, have surprisingly similar observations and insights. This across-the-board consistency implies some kind of "objectivity," at least among the subjective views of people outside Israel, in defining Israelis.

Following is the model I developed by collecting and framing all the data in one pattern, using the word ISRAELI as an acronym to depict the general profile of Israel's business culture:

I Informal

S Straightforward

R Risk-Taking

A Ambitious

E Entrepreneurial

L Loud

I Improvisational

From this book, you will learn how to recognize these characteristics when doing business with Israelis, gain tools for successful intercultural business communication, and find recommendations on working together to achieve business success. Along the way, you may find yourself deeply connecting with the Israelis you work with, and might even gain a few lifelong friends.

> *Everyone wants to understand and trust the individuals they work with. Comprehending the background and nature of the Israeli business culture will increase your confidence in your Israeli colleague, partner, customer, etc., as well as improve your understanding of your own culture.*

"Mastering others is strength. Mastering yourself is true power. If you realize that, you have enough. You are truly rich."

– Lao-Tzu (Tao Te Ching)

A Closer Look: Can We Avoid Cultural Generalizations?

Research on "cultures" deals with groups, and therefore relies on generalizations. As I mentioned earlier, every society has members who do not fit the overall cultural mold. In each culture, there will always be those who behave somewhat differently. Is there a better method of researching cultures, without using generalizations? Can we improve our way of understanding individuals for the sake of creating more productive cross-cultural communication?

Generalization is the first step when we aim to understand any person coming from a different culture. Generalizations are a must in order to delve deeper and, ironically, to comprehend the individual's uniqueness. Professor Stefanie Rathje (2015) from Berlin University of the Arts, however, considers such cultural observations rather dangerous. She holds that this kind of traditional research leads to four major problems (p. 17):

1. Reducing individuals to group statements.

2. Seeing differences as "eternal," without understanding that people change over time, based on ongoing experiences in their personal and professional lives.

3. Insisting on mass cultural gaps, thereby encouraging opposition and out-group dynamics.

4. Pretending that conflicts can be avoided through some kind of knowledge or training.

Prof. Rathje asserts that if we want to solve these problems, we need new training, according to a different cultural paradigm. The first step is to understand that each of us consists of multiple layers; "We are all Michelin men" (p. 20). I, for example, am a woman, 40+ years old, Jewish, a mother, a wife and a consultant, self-employed, Israeli, a daughter, a sister, a traveler, a yoga practitioner and more. Each layer is me, but in each role I communicate with my surroundings in a different way. I am more politically correct as a consultant; very direct and informal as an Israeli; and much more spoiled as a daughter than as a mother.

We are also members of diverse networks. We navigate confidently within our familiar networks, and behave according to known contexts: I dress differently when I go to a yoga class, travel the world or pick up my kids from school. While it's true that I'm an Israeli, I am first and foremost an individual, a person, rather than a "sample."

Networks connect individuals. And when we want to connect to a new network, we often find it very challenging to communicate since we don't feel a sense of interrelatedness or belonging. In other words, language is not the only barrier. When we meet new people from a new network, we can't afford to behave in our customary manner. Sometimes we even need to form new habits in order to build relationships. Meeting new people, especially from different cultures, also gives us an opportunity to examine ourselves and the culture we come from.

I think that despite our multiple layers, and our not being mere representative samples or patterns of our groups, nations or cultures, it is still useful, relevant and necessary to discuss the main characteristics of distinct cultures and—yes—to use generalizations, in order to understand both broad trends and small details. General knowledge of someone's culture is vital for building effective communication with them. Knowing other cultures' clear patterns and main characteristics provides us with the opportunity to understand people in depth, both as a product of their base culture and as unique individuals.

Part 1

ISRAELI BUSINESS CULTURE

BACKGROUND

Part 1: Israeli Business Culture Background

Understanding an individual is simpler when we know his or her family, friends, profession and more. These help us realize what has shaped that person en route to both success and failure in the present. The same is true of any nation; looking at its history, geography and population sheds more light on its main characteristics.

Therefore, before we dive into cross-cultural topics and the main Israeli business culture characteristics, it is vital to discuss important specifics about the State of Israel: its history, borders, military, religion, language and even some amazing inventions. You will learn that although Israel is a young country, it has a long history that influences our daily life and business. Furthermore, the attitudes of the country's founders are clearly manifested in today's reality and results.

"Yesterday affects today, and tomorrow is determined by today."

– David Ben-Gurion, First Prime Minister of the State of Israel

History

Much of what historians know about Israel's ancient history comes from the Hebrew Bible and can be traced back to Abraham, who is considered the father of both Judaism (through his son Isaac) and Islam (through his son Ishmael). The word Israel comes from Abraham's grandson, Jacob, who was renamed "Israel" by the Hebrew God in the Bible.

The Jews reigned over the Land of Israel, with only minor periods of interruption, from approximately 1030 BCE. to 70 CE. For the next several centuries, the land was conquered and ruled by various groups, including the Persians, Greeks, Romans, Crusaders, Egyptians, Ottoman Empire and others.

There was a continual Jewish presence in the Land of Israel throughout the ages, and exiled Jews always aspired to return. In modern times, Zionism (the Jewish people's national movement) sought to reestablish Jewish sovereignty in the homeland; and massive numbers of Jews immigrated to their ancestral holy land and built communities there. Between 1882 and 1903, about 35,000 Jews relocated, and another 40,000 settled in the area between 1904 and 1914. Throughout all this time and up to the creation of the State of Israel, many Arabs from the entire region also migrated to the Holy Land, drawn by the development and favorable conditions created by the Jews, and yet they also violently opposed the Jews' presence there.

When World War I ended in 1918, so did the 400-year reign of the Ottoman Empire, and Great Britain took control over what was then known as Palestine (modern-day Israel, Palestine and Jordan). Later, during the Nazi reign (1933-1945) many Jews living in Europe and elsewhere escaped persecution by finding refuge in Palestine and embracing Zionism. The majority of remaining European Jewry was sent to concentration and extermination camps, and six million of them were slaughtered. After World War II, Holocaust survivors who managed to reach the Holy Land and members of the Zionist movement primarily focused on creating an independent Jewish state.

The horror of the German Nazis' persecution, incarceration and incineration of the European Jewish population had a enormous effect on the state of mind among survivors as well as Jews already living in the Land of Israel. The new mood, perhaps most aptly summed up by the motto **"Never Again"***, determined that the Jewish people cannot rely on anyone but themselves and must defend themselves at all costs. The events of the Holocaust emphasized the importance of the need for a sovereign Jewish country, where members of the ancient people could live without persecution, protect themselves and powerfully stand against any power again seeking to annihilate them. This attitude sums up the consciousness underlying the foundation and existence of the State of Israel.*

In 1948 Israel declared its independence. The Proclamation of Independence stated that the new country would be both Jewish and democratic, an ethnic "melting pot" with immigrants coming from many countries.

(Photo: Pridan, 1958)

The Declaration of the Establishment of the State of Israel, 1948

The Land of Israel was the birthplace of the Jewish people. Here their spiritual, religious and political identity was shaped. Here they first attained to statehood, created cultural values of national and universal significance and gave to the world the eternal Book of Books.

After being forcibly exiled from their land, the people kept faith with it throughout their Dispersion and never ceased to pray and hope for their return to it and for the restoration in it of their political freedom.

Impelled by this historic and traditional attachment, Jews strove in every successive generation to re-establish themselves in their ancient homeland. In recent decades they returned in their masses. Pioneers, defiant returnees, and defenders, they made deserts bloom, revived the Hebrew language, built villages and towns, and created a thriving community controlling its own economy and culture, loving peace but knowing how to defend itself, bringing the blessings of progress to all the country's inhabitants, and aspiring towards independent nationhood.

...

The State of Israel will be open for Jewish immigration and for the Ingathering of the Exiles; it will foster the development of the country for the benefit of all its inhabitants; it will be based on freedom, justice and peace as envisaged by the prophets of Israel; it will ensure complete equality of social and political rights to all its inhabitants irrespective of religion, race or sex; it will guarantee freedom of religion, conscience, language, education and culture; it will safeguard the Holy Places of all religions; and it will be faithful to the principles of the Charter of the United Nations.

...

We extend our hand to all neighbouring states and their peoples in an offer of peace and good neighbourliness, and appeal to them to establish bonds of cooperation and mutual help with the sovereign Jewish people settled in its own land. The State of Israel is prepared to do its share in a common effort for the advancement of the entire Middle East.

...

Placing our trust in the Almighty, we affix our signatures to this proclamation at this session of the provisional Council of State, on the soil of the Homeland, in the city of Tel-Aviv, on this Sabbath eve, the 5th day of Iyar, 5708 (14th May, 1948) (Knesset, n.d.).

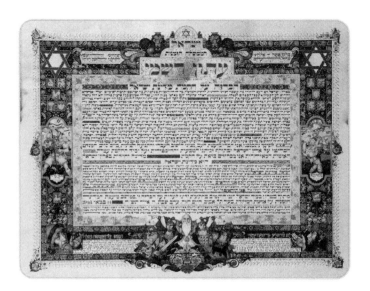

(Photo: Mishella, n.d.)

While this historic event seemed to be a victory for Jews, it also marked the beginning of more violence with the Arabs (see "The War of Independence" in "Military Conflicts"). Following the establishment of the state, immigrants started pouring in from Diaspora communities all over the world. Each community had its own unique characteristics, bringing its special mentality, rituals and culture to the new country.

The first waves of immigration came from Eastern Europe. Later, immigrants came from North Africa and Asia. Much later, a large number of immigrants arrived from the former Soviet Union and Ethiopia. Immigration is an ongoing process. The many Jewish groups living in Israel today are usually broadly categorized according to where their forebears originally came from; i.e., Ashkenazi Jews (from Eastern Europe) and Sephardic Jews (from North Africa and Asia), with a further breakdown into the exact countries of origin.

Demographics

According to the Central Bureau of Statistics (CBS, 2017), Israel presently has 8,793,000 residents. Of those, 74.6% are Jewish (6,556,000 inhabitants), of which 50% are secular and the remainder have different Jewish affiliations; i.e., traditional,

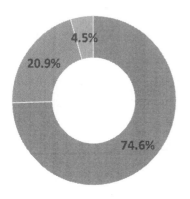

■ Jewish ■ Arabs ■ Others

religious and ultra-Orthodox. Jews in Israel comprise 43% of the world Jewish population. Israeli Arabs account for 20.9% (1,837,000 inhabitants) of the Israeli population, and "others" (mostly Christians, Druze, Samarians and Circassians) for the remaining 4.5 % (400,000 inhabitants).

The current number of residents is almost ten times more than at the time the State of Israel was established: 8,793,000 as opposed to 806,000. During 2017 alone, the population grew by a rate of 1.9%. Fully 82% of the growth stemmed from natural reproduction—more births and fewer deaths, and the remaining 18% from the balance of international migration; the number of immigrants to Israel were greater than the number of émigrés leaving Israel. The population of Israel is projected to reach 11.3 million by 2035.

- In 2017, 30,000 immigrants arrived in Israel, 27.1% of them from Russia, 25.5% from Ukraine, 13% from France and 9.8% from the United States.

- Most immigrants come to Israel out of a desire to reunite with their families and to live as Jews in the Jewish State. See the figure below.

Reasons for Immigration

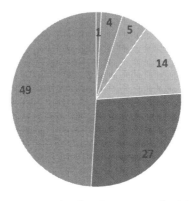

- Sense of personal safety in country of origin
- Professional and economic opportunity in Israel
- The economic situation in country of origin
- The desire for a fresh start
- The desire to live as a Jew in the Jewish state
- Family unification

(Zeltzer-Zubida & Zubida, 2012)

There is no "one-size-fits-all" culture. Individuals are different. Nonetheless, they can have much in common. Israel is a young nation comprised of citizens who arrived – or whose forebears arrived – in Israel with high aspirations for success in the new state. Newcomers continue to arrive in hordes.

Borders

Israel is bordered by Egypt in the south, Jordan in the east, Syria in the northeast and Lebanon in the north. Between Israel, Egypt and the Mediterranean coast lies the Hamas-controlled Gaza Strip. In the central mountain range between Israel and Jordan are the mountains of Judea and Samaria (also known as the West Bank), which are jointly controlled by Israel and the Palestinian Authority. In the northeast is the Israel-controlled Golan Heights, over which Syria has continued to claim sovereignty ever since Israel conquered the territory during the Six Day War in 1967.

Business in Israel is greatly impacted by the fact that it is a small geographical area surrounded and blocked by largely hostile neighbors. Israel's size is 20,770 sq. km, populated by just over eight million people. When Israelis wish to succeed in business, they automatically have to think globally. They can't just hop in the car and sell to their adjacent neighbors, like many people in Europe do. They have to fly by airplane to far-off destinations.

Israelis know that in order to prosper in business they need to:

1. *Practice English as an unofficial second language after Hebrew.*

2. *Conceive global products from the earliest planning and development stages.*

IDF – Israeli Defense Forces

Due to the uncertainty and potential threats inherent in its geography, Israel employs a policy of mandatory conscription for its citizens. Service in the Israel Defense Forces (IDF) is compulsory for men and women. The militarization of the state greatly affects civilian business society, as strong ties frequently exist between military officers and the Israeli business community.

Israeli military researchers call these connections the "security network" (Barak & Sheffer, 2013). The term refers to present and retired military personnel who eventually integrate into roles in the political and business worlds thanks to knowing other ex-military members of the Israeli elite. Individuals with strong network ties take advantage of this informal, non-hierarchical "old boys' club" to facilitate each other's often meteoric rise in various civilian realms.

The term protektzia is Israeli slang for "pulling strings" or "using personal connections." It is similar to the "networking" discussed above but applies to all Israelis in all realms of life, certainly including business, regardless of their army past. It ranges from cutting in line at a store when you see someone you know at the front, to being hired as a contractor for a project because the CEO is your neighbor's son. "Protektzia" can be reasonably innocent (although arguably unfair) but at times also reflects nepotism and shady arrangements. In any case, it is a fact of life in Israel.

Here are some examples of former officers who fill leading positions in the Israeli business and political arenas:

<u>Yoav Galant</u>: Upon retiring from the IDF with the rank of major-general, he was named CEO of Nammax Oil and Gas Corporation. After leaving that position in 2014 due to failed drilling efforts, he became the Minister of Construction in the 34th Israeli government in 2015.

<u>Eliezer ("Chiney") Marom</u>: Formerly a vice-admiral who commanded the Israel Navy, he now serves as the Chairman of the Israel Airports Authority's Board of Directors.

<u>Eli Glickman</u>: A past colonel in the Israeli Navy's Shayetet 13 (the Israeli equivalent of Navy Seals), he became the CEO of the Israel Electric Corporation, until his resignation in September 2014.

These successful individuals and many like them bring their military experience into the business world. As a result, many IDF norms and values have become part of the civilian sphere:

- Courage in confrontational situations (battle, daily life or business).

- Ability to improvise: In the military, Israelis learn to plan courses of action, but are also taught that any plan is subject to change at any moment, so they develop adaptability and how to quickly come up with alternatives whenever necessary.

- Trust in one's superior (commander or manager).

- Ability to assume responsibility.

- Teamwork: "All for one and one for all."

Unit 8200 is the IDF's Signal Intelligence Gathering and Decryption Unit (SIGINT), a subdivision of the Intelligence Corps. It is most famous for the leaders of national and global high-tech industries who once served among its ranks.

Here is a partial list of the unit's nationally and globally successful graduates:

Gil Shwed and Shlomo Kramer, founders of Check Point
Tomer Barel, CEO of PayPal Israel and COO of PayPal International
Shlomo Tirosh, a founder of Gilat Satellite Networks
Ronen Barel, CEO of Ernst & Young, Israel

An article published in The Guardian states: "Israel's Unit 8200 has spawned more technology millionaires than many business schools" (Kalman, 2013). In July 2013, former IDF Chief of General Staff Benny Gantz awarded the unit special recognition for its "outstanding and paramount achievements in the operational activity of the IDF."

An interesting example of how the military mindset influences all other aspects of life in Israel comes through in an article published in USA Today, titled "NBA coach David Blatt compares basketball coaches to fighter pilots" (Schwartz, 2015). David Blatt is an Israeli-American professional basketball coach. He immigrated to Israel in 1981 and served in the Israel Defense Forces (IDF). Blatt chalked up numerous achievements, including coaching Maccabi Tel Aviv to win the 2014 EuroLeague championship. After years of playing and coaching in Israel, he coached the Cleveland Cavaliers from 2014 to 2016.

When Blatt was asked by ESPN's Dave McMenamin about facing criticism on the job, Blatt compared his work as a coach to a fighter pilot, saying that both jobs require making many split-second, critical decisions. USA Today called Blatt's analogy "one of the most ridiculous comparisons in coaching history," but for Israelis it makes a lot of sense. Almost all Israeli citizens serve in the military. Many successful individuals also bring their military experience and idioms into the business world. It naturally follows that Israeli business culture draws many analogies and idioms from IDF concepts and jargon.

In American culture it's considered normal and acceptable to use sports expressions in the business world; and army expressions are the Israeli equivalent. For example: Israelis often say "aiming for the target" to refer to striving to reach a goal, whereas Americans might say "driving it home" in a similar context. Israelis need to "know the borders" while Americans want to understand "the ballpark figure." Israelis see negotiations as a "tough battle" with only one winner, while Americans might view them more as a "league" where more than one team can play and succeed.

Different cultures express themselves in different ways, which is liable to lead to misunderstandings. It is vital strategy (or "game-changing," in American lingo) to have knowledge of your business associate's culture before doing business with them.

> *The influence of military experience on Israelis is not uniform. Some Israelis serve in auxiliary or low-ranking positions and for many of them the army has little subsequent effect on their lives. From research I conducted during my MA studies at Bar-Ilan University as part of a course titled "Army and Society," I discovered that the higher an individual's position in the military, the more significance his service bears on his later life. I, for example, served as a physical fitness instructor for various combatants in the navy, where I learned to stretch my limits and not give up. However, the influence of my army experiences in the long run was less impactful on my life than for someone who, say, takes a naval officers' course and serves as captain on an Israel Navy ship, responsible for commanding a crew of young sailors and dealing with various complex challenges at sea.*

Civil-military relations researcher Rebecca Schiff (1992) claims that Israel is a unique society in which there is no separation between:

1. Civilian and military life

2. Religion and state

3. Private and public

Indeed, Israel is a distinctive nation. It has a people's army, in which citizens serve to protect their homeland. After completing high school, young people in most other countries embark on independent lives of work or study, and continue building up themselves and their skills. At age 18 Israeli youngsters become uniform-wearing soldiers who labor along with their comrades for a cause larger than themselves – defending the State of Israel. This practical and mental experience at such a young age heavily influences the rest of their adult and professional lives.

Israel became a mission-oriented society
in both thought and deed.

Religion

The word Judaism (*Yehadut* in Hebrew) comes from the religion of citizens in the Biblical Kingdom of Judah (*Yehuda*), thus they are Jews (*Yehudim*). Worldwide Jews number 14 million people. Almost half of them live in Israel. As a state with a Jewish majority, Israel is utterly exceptional. To outsiders, it sometimes seems odd, as they are used to Jews being a small minority in other countries.

In Israel, the 68% of Jews who are non-believers or do not observe all of Judaism's religious precepts are considered secular. This number includes many who feel a connection to their heritage and are committed to the religion's principles and family/holiday customs without strictly adhering to all the mitzvahs. This leaves 32% of Israeli Jews who self-identify as religious according to various streams of Judaism. They may be characterized as striving to follow Jewish law to the letter, and as culturally conservative in their way of life and modest in their dress. The ultra-Orthodox among them comprise just 9% of the Jewish Israeli population (Kolodetsky, 2017).

"Hasidic ultra-Orthodox Jewish children look on in a crowd of Hasidim,
while wearing fur hats and silk clothes"
(Photo: Cohen, n.d.)

But the fact remains that Israel is a Jewish state. And although so much of the population is defined as secular, religion still plays an integral part in residents' lives.

Religious   Secular

We have our own calendar based on Jewish holidays (for more information on the holidays, see the end of this chapter). Religion influences almost every aspect of daily life. The Jewish Sabbath ("Shabbat" in Hebrew) begins late Friday afternoon and ends after sundown on Saturday. Most businesses are closed during this time period, as well as public transportation and nationwide supermarket chains. Sunday is a regular working day for Israelis, and the first day of the work week. Israeli culture simply cannot be separated from Jewish identity.

Language

Hebrew is the official national language of the State of Israel. Hebrew was also the language spoken in the Land of Israel during Biblical times. Over time and especially in the Diaspora, Hebrew came to be considered the Holy Tongue, suitable for prayer and not everyday conversation. Other languages, such as Yiddish, Ladino and Aramaic, were used by Jews for secular communication. In the 19th century, with the rise of modern Zionism as part of the European nationalism movement, Hebrew began to be reintroduced into daily life. Eliezer Ben-Yehuda revived the Hebrew language by renewing and adapting words from the Hebrew Bible as well as coining many new words, mostly inspired by terms in Romance languages. Thus the French "avion" for airplane became "aviron" in Hebrew, and the English "brush" was Hebraicized as "mivreshet."

Today some ten million people speak Hebrew, but only five million as their mother tongue. Moreover, the Hebrew language has only about 70,000 words, whereas English boasts approximately a million words. With fewer words to choose from and consequently fewer nuances in the language, it also might take several sentences more to convey the same idea in Hebrew than in English.

The American, British, Canadian and Australian cultures place a much higher emphasis on details than Israeli culture, perhaps because the rich English language enables and reflects a focus on precision. For example, when saying in Hebrew that something is great, excellent or wonderful there is a much smaller vocabulary to choose from, as Hebrew lacks equivalents for the English options of magnificent, terrific, stupendous and so on.

Hebrew is constantly adopting non-Hebrew words. With the technological developments of the past decades, many Israelis have simply added English words to their lexicon. Words such as CD, laptop, deadline, chip, roadmap and others have become part of the Hebrew language. As part of the global community, Israeli businesspeople especially seem to prefer international terms over words coined locally by the Academy of the Hebrew Language.

However, Israelis (like people in many other cultures) also enjoy hearing Hebrew words spoken by non-Israelis. Here is a short list of basic phrases:

English	Hebrew
Yes	*Ken*
No	*Lo*
Good evening	*Erev tov*
Good morning	*Boker tov*
Good night	*Laila tov*
Hello, Goodbye, Peace	*Shalom*
Thank you	*Toda*
Please, You're welcome	*Be'vakasha*
How are you doing?	*Mah nishmah?*
Everything is okay	*Hakol beseder*

Life-Changing Israeli Inventions

Israel is a young (70 years old at the time of this writing), small country (roughly the same size as New Jersey!), yet Israelis have enjoyed tremendous international success in a variety of fields. It is no exaggeration to say that Israeli inventions have brought about significant changes in the world. Following are some examples:

Smart Cars

Mobileye was established in 1999 and is the global leader in the development of vision technology for Advanced Driver Assistance Systems (ADAS) and autonomous driving. The vision is to improve on-road safety and reduce collisions. In March 2017, Intel acquired Mobileye for $15.3 billion. This deal is the largest exit in Israel's high-tech industry to date. Intel expects the driverless market to be worth as much as $70 billion by 2030.

Applications

ICQ was the first instant messaging application, long before Facebook Messenger or Slack. ICQ was developed by the Israeli founders of Mirabilis: Yair Goldfinger, Arik Vardi, Sefi Vigiser and Amnon Amir. Its success led AOL to purchase Mirabilis for $407 million in 1998. At the time, this was the highest ever price paid for an Israeli high-tech company.

<u>**Waze**</u> is an Israeli crowdsourced social navigation GPS application developed by Ehud Shabtai, Amir Shinar and Uri Levine. It works by blending GPS with the smartphone user community. In 2014, Waze was acquired by Google for over a billion dollars!

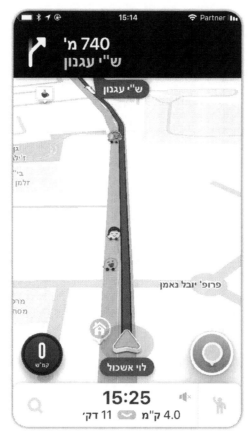

(Waze screenshot)

Defense Systems

Iron Dome is an anti-rocket mobile defense solution developed by Israel's Rafael Advanced Defense Systems and Israel Aircraft Industries. The Israeli companies Elta and mPrest were respectively responsible for the radar system and the command & control system. Iron Dome functions in all weather conditions and is able to respond to multiple simultaneous threats. The system's success rate during Operation Protective Edge in 2014 was over 90%. It has won global acclaim, and several countries have expressed interest in acquiring the technology.

(Photo: IDF/Matanya, 2011)

Xaver products were established in 2004 by the Israeli company Camero-Tech Ltd., one of the world's leading providers of sense-through-the-wall (STTW) solutions. The system enables users to observe multiple objects, whether moving and stationary, concealed behind walls or barriers. It uses advanced micro-power radar technology and offers a unique tactical solution for a variety of military, law enforcement, and homeland security applications. On January 2012, SK Group acquired Camero, which continues to operate under its own name.

Healthcare Products

ReWalk is a wearable robotic exoskeleton that enables individuals with spinal cord injury (SCI) to stand upright and move about. The company ReWalk Robotics was founded by Dr. Amit Goffer, whose own situation as a quadriplegic inspired him to develop a product that would help people with spinal cord injuries walk again. Over the past decade, ReWalk Robotics has grown from a small research and development startup based in Israel to an international company with branches in the U.S., Germany and Israel.

PillCam is a pill-sized camera manufactured by Given Imaging. It is used to monitor and diagnose disorders of the gastrointestinal tract without sedation or invasive endoscopic procedures. Given Imaging was founded in 1998 and acquired by Covidie in March 2014, then only a few months later acquired by Medtronic. Today more than two million patients have already experienced the benefits of PillCam capsule endoscopies.

Agriculture

Smart Dripper is an irrigation pipe accessory that releases water in small spurts. Its development led to a global revolution in irrigation and fertilization methods, and impacted worldwide agriculture. Invented by Israeli engineer Simcha Blass and his son Yeshayahu, the new irrigation systems were further developed and distributed by their company, Netafim, which has become the world's largest irrigation systems producer. On Israel's 50th Independence Day, the Smart Dripper was named the country's "Invention of the Decade."

Cherry Tomatoes – The common variety consumed today was first created in Israel by a development group led by Prof. Nachum Keidar and Prof. Chaim Rabinovitch of the Hebrew University's Faculty of Agriculture, Rehovot Campus, in cooperation with the HaZera company. The cherry tomato was conceived of as a healthy snack that could be conveniently eaten while watching TV. Indeed, the original name was "television tomato," but its similarity to a cherry led to the present name, and cherry tomatoes are consumed all over the world.

Hardware

Disk-on-Key is a USB device that acts as an external hard drive, using flash memory and enabling file transfers to and from the host. It was invented by M-Systems, an Israeli company founded by Dov Moran. M-Systems was ultimately acquired by SanDisk in 2006 for $1.3 billion. The product's Israeli name, "Disk-on-Key" has become a generic term for this important new technology. In other countries, you can find the same device under other names such as Flash Drive, USB Stick or Thumb Drive.

All these inventions, along with many others, were developed by Israelis and occupy dominant places on the international market. Israeli brainpower, ideation and business prowess are obviously considerable and well worth the effort of navigating business connections with Israelis.

A Closer Look: VIP Extended Tour

Government and Politics

The Israeli government is the executive branch of the State of Israel. It is headed by the prime minister and its members are government ministers, whom the prime minister has the authority to appoint and dismiss. The government holds authority over most national and public aspects of the country, and includes government ministries entrusted with various realms: Ministry of Defense (including the IDF and security industries), Ministry of Finance, Ministry of Foreign Affairs, Ministry of Economics, Ministry of Education, Ministry of Health and many others.

The prime minister heads the executive branch of the state and wields the highest authority in the Israel system of government. The current prime minister and most powerful figure in Israeli politics is Benjamin Netanyahu. He is the second longest-serving Prime Minister in Israel's history after David Ben-Gurion (and if his current government lasts a full term, he will hold first place in that regard).

The Current Prime Minister of Israel, Benjamin Netanyahu, 2009-present
(Photo: US State Dept., 2018)

The Knesset is the representative and legislative body of the State of Israel, numbering 120 elected members. The present Knesset is the 20th in Israeli history. Israel's system of government is a parliamentary democracy. Citizens vote for party lists of candidates, and the winning party forms the government, usually by coalition. Its head becomes the prime minister and other party and coalition members are appointed ministers. The government derives its power and authority from the Knesset, and the Knesset regularly monitors the government. The Knesset also has the power to topple the government through a no-confidence vote.

(Photo: The World in HDR, n.d.)

The president of Israel is the head of state but, since Israel is a parliamentary democracy, the position is primarily ceremonial and symbolic – an expression of national unity. The job is usually the individual's last position following a long political career.

Reuben (Ruby) Rivlin, 10th President of the State of Israel, 2014-present
(Photo: Gideon/GPO, 2017)

Shimon Peres, 9th President of the State of Israel, 2007-2014
(Photo: World Economic Forum, 2005)

Politics in Israel

The country has always struggled with complex political issues while maneuvering between sectoral groups and security challenges. Politics in Israel begin with the form of government and are greatly affected by the delicate social fabric. As a parliamentary democracy, Israel suffers from a multiplicity of political parties due to the "melting pot" nature and structure of Israeli society. Among the prominent sectors are ultra-Orthodox, secular and national-religious Jews, and Arabs.

Politics in Israel swing between internal social-financial issues and security issues, including those evoking fear of an existential threat. The security conflicts form a superstructure for political division in Israel, creating major blocs of right, left and center. The social-political left is perceived as more compromising on the core issues of the Israel-Arab conflict, whereas the right is considered more rigid. The political center in Israel attempts to be a balancing force between left and right.

The government is currently ruled by the Likud party, a Zionist faction on the right of the political map, headed by Prime Minister Benjamin Netanyahu.

Military Conflicts

Since its establishment, the State of Israel has been through seven wars and two Intifadas, as well as numerable military conflicts that are not officially defined as wars but most certainly comprise part of the complex armed struggle between Israel and the Arabs.

The War of Independence was started by Arab nations and Arabs living in Israel in 1948, on the day after the state was proclaimed, in an attempt to prevent the establishment of the State of Israel. Most Palestinian Arabs call Israel's Independence Day *Nakba* – "the catastrophe." Despite the infancy of its statehood, Israel succeeded in preserving its existence and prevailing in a war waged on many different fronts, including against reinforcement troops sent by Iraq, Jordan, Syria, Lebanon and Egypt. In the course of the war six hundred thousand Arabs fled the country, and hundreds of Arab villages were destroyed. In response to the proclamation, approximately six hundred thousand Jews were expelled from Arab countries and made their way to the new Jewish state.

The Sinai Campaign (Operation Kadesh) in 1956 took place in response to the Egyptian blockade denying Israeli ships access to the Suez Canal. Israel, in cooperation with the United Kingdom and France, attempted to conquer the Sinai Peninsula and take over the canal. Israel eventually retreated due to international pressure, but the campaign was successful: the Straits of Tiran were opened and Israeli ships could reach their port in Eilat.

The Six-Day War on June 5-10, 1967, was sparked by Egypt's re-closure of the Straits of Tiran. Israel defeated Egypt, Jordan and Syria in just six days. During this brief war, Israel took control of the Gaza Strip and the Sinai Peninsula from Egypt; the West Bank and the Old City of Jerusalem from Jordan; and the Golan Heights from Syria.

The War of Attrition in 1969 took place between Israel and Egypt. It started out as an Egyptian initiative to weaken Israel by violating the cease-fire agreement that had put a stop to the Six Day War. It was Egyptian President Nasser who named the war, which actually ended up tiring out both sides.

The Yom Kippur War in 1973 took place following the euphoria that reigned in Israel in the wake of the Six-Day War. The Arab nations, led by Egypt and Syria, wished to restore their lost honor. Israel ignored the early signs, and was caught by surprise. Egypt and Syria launched air strikes against Israel on the High Holiday of Yom Kippur (see "Israeli-Jewish Holidays"), and Israel suffered heavy losses and casualties for two weeks, until the UN adopted a resolution to stop the war.

The First Lebanon War (Operation Peace for Galilee) in 1982 occurred mostly on Lebanese territory, between Israel and Syria as well as Palestinian organizations based in Lebanon that were carrying out attacks in Israel and other countries.

First Palestinian Intifada (usually translated as "uprising," from an Arabic word literally meaning "shaking off") in 1987-1991. In the preceding months, the number of violent incidents between the Palestinians and Israel had been increasing: murdered Israeli soldiers, stabbings, the killing of terrorists. The extremism of the Israeli right and Islamic fundamentalists led to spontaneous riots. When tensions escalated rather than dying out over time, the IDF sent massive troops into the West Bank and the Gaza Strip to suppress the riots.

After four years of uprising and hundreds of deaths, the Israeli and Palestinian leaders – then Prime Minister Yitzhak Rabin, Foreign Minister Shimon Peres and Chairman of the Palestinian

Authority Yasser Arafat – met in Oslo and signed a ceasefire. The three of them were awarded the Nobel Peace Prize of 1994 for signing the Oslo Accords and for their efforts to create peace in the Middle East.

Nobel Peace Prize laureates for 1994 in Oslo:
(L-R) PLO Chairman Yasser Arafat, FM Shimon Peres, PM Yitzhak Rabin
(Photo: Yaakov/GPO, 1994)

Second Palestinian Intifada in 2000-2005 – At first the Palestinian resistance included protests of varying degrees of violence, but they quickly evolved into widespread mass suicide attacks against citizens of the State of Israel. Of the 516 Israelis murdered and 3,428 injured in 144 suicide attacks, 70% were civilians. Israel carried out over 20,000 acts of reprisal.

The Second Intifada almost completely defeated the Oslo Accords of 1993, and escalated the conflict to a level that hadn't been seen for decades. It also caused a recession in Israel and a severe blow to the Palestinian economy. Despite a general consensus that the Second Intifada ended (thanks to a drastic decline in violence), the date of its conclusion is debatable as there was no defining event that led to its completion.

Second Lebanon War in 2006 – Israel went to war with Hezbollah, a militant Shiite Islamic group in Lebanon. The war began with a premeditated Hezbollah attack on the border, during which three IDF soldiers were killed and two others were abducted. Israel found itself under heavy artillery shelling and responded with a massive assault, first by the air force and later by ground forces as well against Hezbollah troops in Southern Lebanon. A UN-negotiated ceasefire ended the conflict after 34 days of fighting.

Hamas Wars (or Gaza-Israel Conflict) in 2006-2014 – Israel has repeatedly been subjected to attacks from Hamas, a Sunni Islamist militant group that assumed Palestinian power in Gaza in 2006 and split with the Fatah party in the West Bank. The more significant conflicts took place in Gaza: Operation Cast Lead in 2008-2009, Operation Pillar of Defense in 2012 and Operation Protective Edge in 2014.

Climate and Geography

The Land of Israel is situated in the Middle East and technically belongs to the Asian continent, although it virtually lies at a crossroads between Asia, Europe and Africa. It boasts a Mediterranean climate, with two dominant seasons: a rainy winter (November to May) and a humid summer (June-October). The Israeli winter does not resemble the European or North American winter, and feels like spring to many visitors.

In such a tiny country (22,770 sq. km), mountains, plains and desert are often minutes apart. You can cross by car from the Mediterranean Sea in the west to the Dead Sea (the lowest point on earth: 430.5 m (1,412 ft) below sea level) in the east in 90 minutes. Driving from the city of Haifa in the north to Eilat at the country's southernmost tip takes only six hours.

Despite its small size, the country is customarily divided into three different climate zones:

- Mediterranean – most of the northern and central regions, characterized by a hot, dry summer, fickle transition seasons and a cold, rainy (occasionally even snowy) winter with over 400 mm (16") of annual precipitation.

- Semi-arid prairie – halfway between Mediterranean and desert climes, and impossible to precisely define the borderline since the annual rainfall can vary wildly from year to year in prairie climate areas, such as Beersheba, for example from 200 to 400 mm (8-16").

- Desert – most of southern Israel, which actually comprises part of the world's subtropical desert belt, is arid and has low precipitation for most of the year, with no more than 200 mm (8") annually.

Surface water in Israel is found mostly in the Sea of Galilee (Kinneret) – 164 sq. km (63 sq. mi), the Dead Sea – 310 sq. km (120 sq. mi) and the Jordan River – 251 sq. km (97 sq. mi).

Main Cities: Jerusalem and Tel Aviv – Two Extremes of Holy and Secular

Jerusalem (population 865,720) is the capital of the State of Israel. The city is over 3,000 years old, counting from the time King David made it his kingdom's capital. The United States has finally formally recognized Jerusalem as Israel's capital and in May 2018 moved its embassy there from Tel Aviv, with some other countries following suit.

Jerusalem is a combination of old and new elements. The Old City contains ancient culture and mystery; and the new part of the city features advanced technology and modern society. Jerusalem is sacred to the three principle monotheistic faiths: Judaism, Christianity and Islam. The city is also home to Israel's government, the Knesset, the Supreme Court and Hebrew University.

As of 2015, 63% of the Jerusalem population is Jewish, of which 66% identifies as religiously observant or ultra-Orthodox Jews, almost equally split, and 34% as secular (Jerusalem Institute,

2017, p. 2). Thus the character and atmosphere of the Jewish parts of the city are decidedly affected by the religious majority. In practical terms, for example, all passersby are expected to dress modestly in some neighborhoods. Throughout the Sabbath many entertainment spots are closed, the buses don't run and some areas are blocked off to traffic.

(Photo: JekLi, n.d.)

<u>Tel Aviv</u> (population 432,892) is the economic and cultural center of Israel. The city contains the financial center, the Tel Aviv Stock Exchange, international embassies and consulates, the largest newspapers' offices, the Habima National Theater, the Philharmonic Orchestra and other major cultural bodies.

Tel Aviv was originally built on sand dunes, so it was deemed unprofitable to develop agriculture in the city. Maritime trade was also ruled out since that industry was already concentrated in Haifa. Consequently, Tel Aviv evolved as a center of science and technology and, starting already back in the 1980s, slowly became one of the most booming high-tech hotspots in the Middle East, even in the entire world. Nicknamed "Silicon Wadi," Tel Aviv is ranked second in industry importance, right after California's famous Silicon Valley (Rabi, 2015). Over the years, numerous global tech companies, such as Microsoft, Google, Facebook and many others, have chosen to set up development centers in the greater Tel Aviv area.

In Tel Aviv, where 92% of the population is Jewish (World Population Review, 2018) and 87% of the Jewish population identifies as secular (Jerusalem Institute, 2017, p. 2), sometimes it is almost possible to forget you are in Israel. The 11% religiously observant and 2% ultra-Orthodox (ibid) are all but invisible. Although it has 544 active synagogues, Tel Aviv is primarily a beach town, the "city that never sleeps" according to its marketing slogan, one of the most LGBT-friendly cities worldwide and the vegan capital of the world.

(Photo: Todorovic, n.d.)

Near Independence Hall in Tel Aviv is a statue of Meir Dizengoff astride his horse. Dizengoff was elected Tel Aviv's first mayor and served two long (non-consecutive) terms between 1911 and his death in 1936. His unique personality greatly impacted the character of the entire city. Even though Tel Aviv in those days was more like a small town, he envisioned a modern, dynamic Hebrew metropolis and helped shape it accordingly. Dizengoff once said (qtd in Finkler, 2018):

> *"Not the houses, streets and buildings make up a city – but the qualities of its residents: the language, love of work and creativity, equality, freedom, belief in their own powers, and the will to live a life of honor and stand on their own. Preserve our national ideals, because the future of our city lies therein. Long live Jewish genius! Long live the city of Tel Aviv!"*

Statue of Meir Dizengoff. In the background: Dizengoff's former home, where the Jewish state was proclaimed on May 14, 1948, now a public museum called Independence Hall, located at 16 Rothschild St., Tel Aviv.
(Photo: Teicher, 2009)

Cuisine

Israel is a relatively young nation whose cooking tradition is still evolving. As a country of immigrants, the cuisine that is considered Israeli consists of diverse foods that have crossed their borders of origin and become an integral part of the Israeli kitchen; for instance, shakshuka (from the North African Jewish ethnic group), malawach (Yemenite-Jewish), cottage cheese (North American), schnitzel (Ashkenazi), humous/  tahini (Mediterranean) and others. The ingathering of the exiles, with their talent for innovation and daring, has also given rise to a delicious fusion cuisine abounding in exciting, imaginative dishes.

(Photo: McClean , n.d.)

This was not always the case. The culture in Israel used to be one of austerity, stemming mainly from Zionist ideology that was partially expressed by a modest way of life. Cooking was purely functional and economical in the past, with no flamboyance or overindulgence. Over the years, and partly due to seeing what was happening in the rest of the Western world, the need for normalcy and quality of life grew stronger in Israel.

In addition, Jewish culture has always placed a high emphasis on family, social and holiday gatherings, with food as a central feature. The multitude of get-togethers and ethnic groups in Israel translates into gastronomic diversity and creativity. With

Europe fighting terrorism and the refugee crisis, and the United States in a flurry around the Trump presidency, tiny Israel, swamped as it is with conflicts from within and without, is seeking some quiet comfort and finding it in food. In Israel, we eat, we feed others and we talk about food. All the time.

So, just as Israel has become a high-tech superpower, it has also turned into a major culinary player. The Israeli kitchen now occupies a prominent place on the world's food map. Israeli chefs have become celebrities on TV and in the gossip columns, and their excellent restaurants, both local and worldwide, are prestigious, expensive and packed with happy diners. International foodies define Israeli cuisine as "provocative-stylized." The ingredients' freshness, intriguing combinations and the relatively simple manner of preparation all set it apart.

Israelis have taken traditional and multicultural food and, through their characteristic innovativeness, made it modern and, most importantly, original.

Israeli Jewish Holidays

Judaism uses a lunar calendar, which is why religious holidays fall on different Gregorian calendar dates each year. Not only that, the Jewish day starts at sundown, so each holiday actually starts the night before, which is called "--- Eve." There are joyous holidays as well as days of fasting, mourning and soul searching. Following are the main national holidays in Israel:

Rosh Hashanah (meaning the beginning—literally the head—of the year) is a two-day celebration occurring in September or sometimes October, depending on the Hebrew calendar. The Jewish New Year is traditionally considered the Day of Judgment, on which the Almighty assesses each person's behavior over the preceding year, and determines what will befall them in the coming year. This is a high holiday of festive family meals and prayers, with all religious and even many secular Israelis attending synagogue. Businesses are closed, and many employers give each of their employees a nice gift or gift card in honor of this holiday.

Yom Kippur (Day of Atonement), ten days after Rosh Hashanah, is considered by Jews to be the holiest and most solemn day of the year. As it is a day of repentance and forgiveness, the Torah requires Jews to "suffer," mostly in the form of refraining from food and drink, bathing and intimate relations. Jewish people traditionally observe this holy day with a 25-hour period of fasting and intensive prayer, often spending most of the day in synagogue services. All businesses are closed, traffic comes to a virtual halt, and the streets swarm with pedestrians and bicyclists.

Sukkot (also known as Tabernacles or the Feast of Booths), four days after Yom Kippur, is one of the three pilgrimage festivals mentioned in the Bible. The holiday lasts seven days in Israel, whereas work is forbidden on the first day and the last, which is the joyful holiday of **Simchat Torah**. Certain work is permitted on the five Intermediate Days of Sukkot, known in Hebrew as *Hol Hamoed*. Families and many organizations construct their own *sukkah* – a special kind of booth. Throughout the holiday, meals are eaten inside the *sukkah* and many people sleep there as well. It is considered a *mitzvah* (good deed) for every Jew to sit in the *sukkah* during the holiday and to host guests there as well.

(Photo: Alefbet, (n.d.)

The expression "after the holidays" is quite common in Israel. The high holidays and vacation time of Rosh Hashana, Yom Kippur and Sukkot are so close together that very few full work days remain during the Hebrew month of Tishrei, which falls sometime in September–October. This entire period is usually devoted to family, as people basically go from one holiday to a weekend to another holiday. Customers and colleagues abroad often don't understand why Israelis seem to be unavailable and barely at work during this time, and why most requests are answered with "Wait until after the holidays!" It's a good thing that the next holiday— Hanukkah—doesn't come along for another couple of months.

<u>Hanukkah</u> (or Chanukah) is the eight-day Jewish "Festival of Lights," in November or December, celebrated with a nightly menorah lighting (adding one more candle each night), special prayers and fried foods. The Hebrew word Hanukkah means "dedication," and is thus named because it celebrates the rededication of the Holy (Second) Temple in Jerusalem at the time of the Maccabean Revolt in the 2nd century BCE. Schools are closed but most workplaces remain open.

<u>Purim</u> (Festival of Lots) commemorates the salvation of the Jewish people in ancient Persia from the evil government official Haman. Purim is celebrated in early spring with parties, the exchange of gifts baskets and parades. Thousands of people take to the streets, showing off costumes made especially for the holiday (similar to Halloween). There are no particular

work restrictions, yet many parents take the day off to enjoy the festivities with their children.

Passover (Pesach) is an important, biblically proscribed (in 1300 BCE) Jewish holiday and the second of the three pilgrimage festivals. Jews celebrate Passover in spring to commemorate their liberation by God from slavery in ancient Egypt and their freedom as a nation under Moses' leadership. The primary commandments are to refrain from eating leavened products for the duration of the holiday (seven days in Israel) and to hold a festive Seder meal on the first night, including the retelling of the Exodus story. Passover is one of the most widely observed Jewish holidays. Schools are closed for the holiday and workplaces are closed on the first and last days. Employers customarily give some kind of gift to all their employees before this holiday.

Holocaust and Heroism Remembrance Day (Yom HaShoah) is a national memorial day held in April or May to mourn the approximately six million Jews who perished in the Holocaust due to the actions carried out by Nazi Germany and its collaborators, and to commemorate heroic resistance by Jews and "righteous Gentiles" during that period. Places of public entertainment and restaurants are closed by law, starting the night before. Ceremonies are held at schools, military bases and other public and community organizations. At 10:00 a.m., a siren sounds throughout the country and most people cease whatever they are doing, including motorists who stop their cars in the middle of the road, for a minute of solemn reflection.

Memorial Day for the Fallen Soldiers of Israel and Victims of Terrorism (Yom HaZikaron) is Israel's other official memorial day. It takes place one week after Holocaust Remembrance Day and one day before Independence Day, so that all will remember the price the nation has been paying ever since its establishment. Yom HaZikaron is an especially solemn time and marked by ceremonies across the country. It starts the night before, when a one-minute siren is sounded throughout Israel at 8:00 p.m. Everybody stops what they are doing, including cars driving on the highway, and stands silently with head bowed to show their respect and remember the fallen. The following day, a two-minute siren sounds at 11.00 a.m. and again the country stops to remember. Unlike in many other countries, Israel's wars have taken place at home rather than abroad. In such a small country, most people know somebody who died in the country's wars, making Yom HaZikaron an incredibly personal time of remembrance. As of Yom HaZikaron 2017, the total number was 23,544 fallen soldiers and victims of terrorism.

(Photo: SigDesign, n.d.)

Independence Day (Yom HaAtzmaut) is a spring holiday marking the proclamation of the State of Israel at the end of the British Mandate. Almost every city, town and village puts on some sort of celebration and fireworks. The official state ceremony takes place on the preceding evening at Mount Herzl in Jerusalem, marking the end of the solemn Yom HaZikaron and the beginning of the Yom HaAtzmaut festivities. Most people do not work on this holiday, although some buses run and many entertainment spots and restaurants are open. Israelis flock with family and friends to parks and nature spots for barbecues and picnics.

Lag B'Omer is a festive Jewish holiday in May commemorating Rabbi Shimon bar Yochai. On Lag B'Omer Eve, children (supervised by parents) and teens light bonfires. The next day, schools are closed but most workplaces remain open.

Shavuot (Feast of Weeks or Pentecost) is the last of Judaism's three pilgrim festivals. The word Shavuot means "weeks." It falls in May or June and marks the completion of seven weeks after Passover. It was on Shavuot that God gave the Torah—the Hebrew Bible—to the Jewish people on Mount Sinai more than 3,300 years ago. Dairy foods are traditionally eaten at the festive Shavuot holiday meal. Workplaces and schools are closed.

Most of Israel's Jewish citizens, including those who define themselves as secular, observe at least some of the commandments and traditions on the Jewish holidays. Notably, 94% hold a Seder on Passover (Ynet, 2014), 93% light Hanukkah candles (Hacohen, 2010) and 61% fast on Yom Kippur (Nachshoni, 2016).

Summer Vacation: *Less than two months after Shavuot, summer vacation begins (on June 20 for middle and high schools and July 1 for primary schools and kindergartens) and lasts until August 31. Many families in Israel take advantage of this opportunity to go on a long vacation, especially in August, when the heat is particularly difficult as well. Then September comes, marking both the start of a new school year and the approach of the holidays, beginning with Rosh Hashanah. And thus begins a new cycle of work, holidays and vacations, until the next year...*

Part 2

ISRAELI™ BUSINESS CULTURE

CHARACTERISTICS

Part 2: ISRAELI™ Business Culture Characteristics

What is unique about the Israeli business culture? What is the best way of working with Israelis so you will succeed in your business dealings with them?

In this section I present each one of the Israeli characteristic in detail in its diverse manifestations, along with real-life examples and recommendations for optimal behavior when coming into contact with Israelis.

For the past decade I've been asking managers from all over the world – India, China, Japan, Africa, the United States and all of Europe – to share their experiences of working with Israelis. Based on these interviews as well as my vast experience with international organizations, I developed a model describing the seven main characteristics of the Israeli business culture.

My ISRAELI™ model uses the letters of the word "Israeli" as an acronym, with each letter standing for one of Israel's business culture characteristics:

I   Informal

S   Straightforward

R   Risk-Taking

A   Ambitious

E   Entrepreneurial

L   Loud

I   Improvisational

I is for Informal – not just how we dress, but also how we communicate with one another.

S for Straightforward, because we use a direct style of speech.

R is Risk taking, A is Ambitious, and E is Entrepreneurial. These three are interrelated, because an entrepreneur is someone with a great idea who also has the necessary ambition and the willingness to take risks and do whatever it takes to reach their goal.

L stands for Loud, not just our raised voices but also our somewhat aggressive manner and the intense atmosphere in Israel.

And the last I is Improvisational, because we are creative, adaptable and always try to think outside the box.

This part is divided into sections, each devoted to a business characteristic according to the ISRAELI™ model. The true stories, examples, explanations and recommendations are meant to help you develop the cultural mindset that will bridge the cultural gaps and improve your business and interpersonal communication with Israelis. The chapter ends with a handy quick-reference summary of the model along with concise tips.

I Informal

S Straightforward

R Risk-Taking

A Ambitious

E Entrepreneurial

L Loud

I Improvisational

Informal

Tel Aviv beach sculpture of David Ben-Gurion practicing yoga.
(Photo: Teicher, 2015)

Informality in Israeli business culture is expressed in different ways, such as:

• Casual dress in the workplace

• Egalitarian expression of opinions among employees at different levels in an organization

• Familiarity, such as asking personal questions and using nicknames

---

Anecdote:

A global organization's human resource director sent out an email inviting the company employees to a special New Year's event. No dress code was mentioned. The only clues as to the kind of festivity being planned were that it would be held on a boat on the Hudson River in New York, and that cocktails would be served.

Two senior executives from the company's Israeli branch, Rinat and Amos, were flying to New York to attend the party. Rinat, who had more experience with Americans than Amos, first contacted Alexandra, a colleague in the New York office, and asked her what she was planning to wear. Alexandra said she was renting a dress especially for the occasion. The only time most Israeli women would rent a dress is on their wedding day. Nonetheless, Rinat understood the event was important and decided to bring her fanciest dress.

Amos, on the other hand, did not seek any advice. As a senior global director, he had often visited the organization's posh Fifth Avenue office, and company employees were used to seeing him in a suit and tie. As this was to be a social occasion, he felt that dressing informally in denim would give the impression that he was open and accessible.

Several days after the event, Rinat contacted Alexandra. The first thing her New York colleague said was, "Rinat, why in the world did Amos dress like that? It was totally disrespectful!" Rinat tried to explain that Israeli culture is less formal and that Amos wore jeans to express equality and solidarity with the employees. But Alexandra couldn't see it that way. In her eyes, Amos had been discourteous to his New York colleagues.

In many other countries, professionalism is reflected not just through expertise in a particular line of work but also includes other aspects of one's performance, such as proper dress, punctuality and courtesy. Most Israelis dress casually, even at work, and don't ascribe much importance to business attire. They live in a country with a hot climate and dress to feel comfortable. Professionalism is measured primarily by the way a person carries out his work.

A professional dress code is standard in most of the business world, except perhaps in the Silicon Valley where informality is the rule (Schmidl, 2012). While Mark Zuckerberg and others may dress in jeans and sports shirts, some workers would still say that, with all due respect to being "cool" and having billions of dollars, business attire has to convey an air of seriousness and professionalism.

It's also important to remember that different business realms have different customs. For instance, people dress more formally in the financial and legal sectors, in Israel as well, whereas clothing tends to be very cool and trendy in the world of entrepreneurs and high-tech.

Informality in the Israeli business world is furthermore expressed in the way people interact. For instance, in preliminary meetings Israelis might easily ask you questions about your personal life, such as whether you are married or have children. Or they might address you with a nickname. Even Prime Minister Benjamin Netanyahu is called by his nickname, Bibi. Similarly, Moshe Ya'alon – former Minister of Defense and Chief of General Staff – is known as Bogie. Using such monikers gives both sides a feeling of closeness and maybe even friendship. This would be considered positive and usual in tiny Israel, where nearly "everyone knows everyone" or at least have acquaintances in common. Familiarity is typical to the Israeli business culture, in which great importance is attributed to one's network of personal relationships.

Job Interviews

Since Israel is an informal society, job interviews can often start with a spontaneous chat with the head of HR. This little talk might include private subjects like: May I contact your last boss? How much did you make at your last job? And so forth. Non-Israeli candidates are liable to feel very uncomfortable in this kind of situation. Rather than understanding and dealing with the cultural gap, they clam up and the poor interpersonal communication is frustrating for both sides.

3 Tips for Non-Israeli Candidates Applying for a Position in Israeli Companies:

1. Try to allow for spontaneity in the process. Don't think of informal discussion as unprofessional but rather be empathetic to how things are done in another culture. Personality and motivation make a good impression on Israelis. Try to show enthusiasm throughout the interview.

2. Answer direct and personal questions as fully as possible, but if any of them cross a line for you, calmly explain that you're having trouble answering because this type of thing is not discussed in your culture.

3. Leave room for misunderstandings due to culture gaps and language gaps. Since English is a second language for most Israelis, you may have to adjust the phrasing and speed of your speech, and make sure that it was correctly understood.

3 Tips for Israeli Recruiters Interviewing Non-Israelis:

1. Be clear and organized: Send a mail to prospective employees outlining the interview process, including with whom he or she will be meeting, the duration of the process, etc. (A spontaneous, unstructured chat as described above is considered unprofessional in global eyes).

2. Avoid private and personal questions such as regarding age, number of children, former salary, etc.

3. Don't rush to pass judgment: Leave room for misunderstandings due to culture gaps and language gaps.

Here's an excellent example of a recruiting process gone wrong due to cultural gaps:

A global Israeli company decided that their expanding activities in the Philippines mandated opening a local branch there. They thought it best to begin by hiring a Filipino national to serve as the general manager and HR director of the proposed Philippine branch. During their recruitment efforts, they discovered that a qualified Filipina human resources manager just happened to be vacationing with her family in France at that very time.

Israeli informality is best expressed in face-to-face meetings and thinking outside the box. So the Israelis thought it would be nice, as well as a good opportunity, to interview the candidate while she was on her family vacation. The prospective manager, who apparently was very interested in the job, agreed to the meeting. But just an hour before the scheduled time, she called the agency in Israel in a frenzy, saying she wasn't sure it was proper to hold a work meeting during a family holiday both because she didn't have appropriate clothes with her and because it is wrong to mix personal time with professional time!

In the informal Israeli society, people appreciate efforts put in outside regular work hours and also spontaneity. Meeting during vacation time would demonstrate high motivation, which is highly valued in Israel. It would be a good way to gain Israelis' trust. In contrast, the Filipina candidate comes from a much more conservative and hierarchical society that values formality, planning and professionalism. The proposed meeting made her extremely nervous, which in turn made the Israelis nervous that if just the circumstances of the interview were too hard on her, perhaps she would also have difficulty in other situations involving the spontaneous, casual Israeli culture...

Management Style

Geert Hofstede, a well-known researcher in the field of cross-cultural communication, has examined the impact of cultural factors on managerial styles (1991). As part of a study he carried out at IBM branches in different countries in the 70s, Hofstede handed out questionnaires to 72,000 employees asking them about their kinds of work, job satisfaction, the relationship between employees and managers, etc. He found that employers' managerial styles were heavily affected by the culture and social environment of the country in which the branch was located, even though the local workers constituted part of an international company, which might be assumed to have one standardized managerial style.

As a result of his survey analysis, Hofstede developed the term "power distance." Power distance is defined as the degree of importance a culture attributes to status and the extent that status is maintained over time. This criterion includes relations between superiors and subordinates, and relates to questions such as: How much respect is shown to authority figures? Is it acceptable to bypass hierarchy levels in your organization?

Hofstede's system assigned Israel 13 points. This score lies at the very lowest end of the spectrum compared to other countries. Here is the comparison taken from Hofstede's databank:

Power Distance

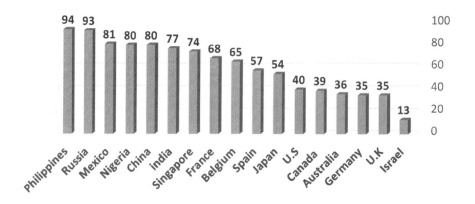

As you can see, Israel is at the tail end on Hofstede's graph. Likewise, in the following graphs in this book, Israel is always at an extreme in comparison to other countries.

From Hofstede's research measuring the power distance in each country, anyone can better understand his/her own behavior and that of others, in order to find the right balance between their own culture standardization and the culture of the locals. For example, the above graph shows Israel with the lowest score (13) and the Philippines with the highest score (94). This tells us that the cultural gap is extremely wide. In the earlier story of the global Israeli company that wished to interview the candidate from the Philippines during her family vacation, we now understand that according to the hierarchical norms in the Philippines, opposing someone more senior in rank or older is not customary, and behavior is based on planning and formality. This is so different from the Israeli culture with its spontaneity, informality, and almost total lack of hierarchy. The Israelis' impulsive request to meet the Filipina candidate in France reveals inconsideration and a lack of cultural awareness. Hofstede's graph paints a clear picture of where we stand regarding hierarchy as opposed to others. It's always important in global interrelations to be aware of the gap and act out of understanding of and empathy for other people's cultures.

In Israel, it is understood that the manager is one of the team. The business culture in Israel is characterized by a low power distance. In other words, **Israelis prefer egalitarian leadership**, where it is acceptable to disagree with the boss or to email/call people several levels above or below you.

Due to Israelis' egalitarian mindset:

• Independence is seen as a virtue and is encouraged

• Superiors are accessible to subordinates

• Employees are empowered by management

• Communication often skips hierarchical lines

• Managers count on their team members' experience

• Employees expect to be consulted and heard

• Respect is earned by proving hands-on expertise

> *Remember:*
>
> *In Israel employees typically communicate in a friendly, open manner with their boss, using a direct, informal style of speech and even giving negative feedback in front of others. But at the end of the day the manager has the last, decisive word. In Israel, a goal-oriented culture, everyone knows that even if the communication style doesn't adhere to hierarchical roles, only one captain leads the ship and makes the final call; otherwise, everyone will drown.*

I once interviewed a German woman living in Israel. In Germany she had been an economic consultant to a large European company; in Israel she is a business consultant. When I asked for her impression of working with Israelis, she answered that she would never want to be an executive in Israel because of the locals' lack of respect for senior managers. In Germany, employees treat their managers with deferential respect and patiently learn from them over time. In Israel, young employees are more daring, and tend to express their opinions freely and confidently, including to their managers. With her German background, this woman would have had difficulty accepting that kind of atmosphere in the workplace.

Similarly, once when I was interviewing a young Chinese man living in Israel, he mentioned that he finds it very strange how Israelis address their managers by their first names. In China, the hierarchy is very clear and is considered highly important, to such an extent that employees call their manager by his job title followed by his last name, e.g., "Manager Wang." You would never hear the equivalent being used in Hebrew!

> *Even in Israel's educational system, authority figures ranging from kindergarten teachers and high school principals through university professors are addressed by their given names. That's how ingrained the low power distance is in the Israeli culture.*

A Closer Look: Israeli Informality on the Job

A Chinese company recently acquired a famous Israeli food industry concern. One of the senior managers from China arrived in Israel to discuss some of the company's ongoing changes. During the meetings, the Israelis kept challenging every step of the discussions to the point that the Chinese manager felt like it was almost impossible to proceed productively. He felt that the Israeli employees lacked respect for him. In Chinese culture, employees show the utmost respect to their seniors. They might confront their colleagues, but never their manager. Although previously aware of the informal Israeli business culture, in which everyone is treated as equals, the Chinese manager found himself having trouble leading his Israeli team.

Advice for managers working with Israelis:

Try to push power down through the organization and step out of the way. This will motivate your Israeli employees and also make them respect you for trusting and challenging them. If possible, minimize the use of titles, addressing your team members by their first names and encouraging them to do the same with you. Help them feel comfortable working with you.

Advice for Israeli managers working with hierarchical cultures:

Allow your employees to address you formally, using Miss, Mrs. or Mr. plus your family name. Also understand that subordinate employees expect and require your approval in order to move forward. If you don't adopt this approach, managers and employees from hierarchical cultures will see you as a weak and ineffective leader, and the business will suffer. Ask your team to meet without you sometimes, to help them feel more comfortable sharing ideas, as well as to gradually encourage independence.

Remember: In today's global business reality, being either an egalitarian leader or a hierarchical leader is insufficient. You need to be both, and to develop your versatility to manage diverse groups. Ultimately, this means it's best to learn how to be flexible and lead in different ways.

The Chain of Command in Crunch Time

In Operation Protective Edge, the war between Israel and Gaza in 2014, IDF 2nd Lt. Hadar Goldin was seized by Hamas soldiers and pulled into an underground tunnel leading back to Gaza. Despite clear IDF directives that soldiers were not to enter tunnels for fear of their being kidnapped, his friend and fellow officer, Lt. Eitan, went into the tunnel to look for Goldin. In an interview given afterwards to the Israeli newspaper Yediot Ahronoth (Yehoshua, 2014), Lt. Eitan said he had asked his superior officer for authorization. "The company commander didn't agree. The battalion commander didn't agree. So I appealed even higher up to get the okay. [The brigade commander] told me, 'Throw a grenade into the tunnel and then go in yourself.'" Lt. Eitan did so and brought out evidence sadly enabling the IDF to confirm Goldin's death.

In the eyes of the Israeli public, Lt. Eitan was a hero due to his courage and willingness to risk his life. The army also awarded him a medal for distinguished service after the war ended. Lt. Eitan had taken an added risk by skipping over his immediate superiors in order to take action. Yet, according to the Israeli mindset, his successful boldness and the final outcome were the most crucial aspects of his conduct.

I   Informal
S   Straightforward
R   Risk-Taking
A   Ambitious
E   Entrepreneurial
L   Loud
I   Improvisational

Straightforward

Direct style

Indirect style

Straightforward behavior includes:

- Direct, candid style of speech

- Dialogue characterized by rapid shifts from one subject to another

- Easy, simple and clear communication

Anecdote:

John, the VP of sales in a high-tech company based in London, has spent the past three months working on his team's targets for the coming year. He calls his team together for a meeting to outline the strategy and goals, explaining each team member's role. John stresses that this is an open discussion and he looks forward to receiving feedback. After John presents his strategy, most of the team express excitement and ask follow-up questions about John's plan.

Yossi, an Israeli sales director on John's team who recently moved to London, has some concerns about the strategy and, unlike the others, voices reservations. He says at the team meeting, "I think it's a mistake to push aside all the smaller deals we've been working on and focus on just a few strategic deals. Small projects will generate higher revenue in the future." John is visibly offended by Yossi's comment and reiterates that the focus for next year is on strategic opportunities and that the whole sales team needs to be on board with this plan.

Two weeks have passed since that meeting, and Yossi feels that John is not consulting him as much he used to. Yossi doesn't understand what happened. With the same straightforwardness and honesty that characterize Israeli culture, Yossi decides to speak directly with his VP and ask John whether there's anything he wants to tell him.

John is tempted to answer Yossi in the diplomatic manner characteristic of British culture, but nonetheless decides to speak with surprising frankness. He explains to Yossi that it is not customary to challenge the manager's strategy in front of subordinates. Astonished, Yossi responds, "But you said it was an open discussion. Didn't you want to hear other opinions?" John explains that his words shouldn't have been taken so literally. He advises that the next time Yossi disagrees with him, he should approach him privately and not make contrary statements in front of the whole team.

Saying What You Mean

Anthropologist Edward T. Hall was the first to categorize the relative straightforwardness of different cultures. In his book *Beyond Culture* (1967), he recommends the terms **low-context culture** and **high-context culture**.

In a high context culture, many things are left unsaid, and one has to infer them with the help of body language and cultural knowledge. It is relatively easy for people from the same culture to understand each other's unarticulated cues and subliminal messages but more difficult for outsiders. According to Hall, the Japanese, for example, have a high-context culture, as do India and China.

In a low context culture, good communication is precise, detailed and simple. Messages are expressed and understood literally, with few hidden or contextual elements. According to Hall, the United States is the lowest-context culture in the world, followed by Canada, Holland and Germany.

The Israeli culture may also appear to be low context, mainly due to its use of direct language. However, I don't think that classification tells the whole story because Israelis also use a lot of body language and shared context among small communities. Moreover, the Hebrew language has only 45,000 words, of which a relatively high percentage can be interpreted in multiple ways depending on the circumstances and tone. For example, the Hebrew word "Shalom" means peace, harmony, wholeness, completeness, prosperity and welfare, and can be used idiomatically to mean both hello and goodbye. Israelis also use a great deal of slang and all this indicates that for non-Israelis to understand what Israelis are saying, they need more than the surface meaning of words.

While Israel is obviously a relatively low context culture, I think it more relevant to isolate the variable of direct or indirect speech and compare that to other countries. In a spectrum ranging from direct to indirect communication in various countries, communication in Israel would undoubtedly be considered the most direct.

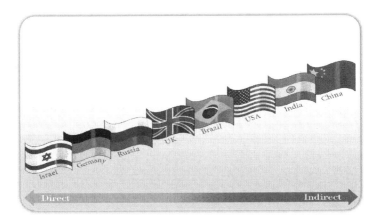

This graph is based on my research interviews with businesspeople from all over the world who have shared their experiences of working with Israelis, as well as on my own years of consulting for international companies.

In Israeli culture you don't have to dig deep to understand other people. What they say is what they mean. When Israelis think you are mistaken, they simply say, "You're wrong." When Israelis invite you to their homes, they expect you to arrive. When you ask for their opinion, they assume you really want it, and give you an honest and straightforward answer. In the local jargon, this style of communication is known as *dugri*.

As mentioned in Part 1, Israel is a country of immigrants who arrived from various places speaking a multitude of languages. Modern Hebrew was formed with the desire to create an official tongue in the Land of Israel, a relatively simple language that new immigrants could acquire. Israelis have to use direct, immediate, easy words and syntax without much fancy diplomacy – the Hebrew language – in order to communicate with each other. It's an integral part of their culture.

On the other hand, cultures that use an indirect style of speech, such as China and India, value tactfulness and ambiguity. In India, for example, hierarchy plays a key role in the business culture. When an employee is asked a question by his boss he will most often answer "Yes." But "Yes" might have various meanings, such as "Yes, I heard you, and I have a totally different opinion," or "Yes, I will do it"...or even "Yes, but I won't do it."

In the United States, a country that uses more diplomatic speech, disagreement with the other can be expressed in a tactful sentence such as, "What you are suggesting sounds interesting. Let's discuss it in the future." This is the kind of evasive remark that Americans learn at an early age. Israelis, who employ a much more direct style of speech, find it very difficult to understand whether such friendly words express a genuine intent to comply or not. They are accustomed to straight talking, which in the eyes of Americans can appear rude and aggressive. We see that an understanding of the cultural context is necessary for understanding what an employee really means by "Yes."

A few years ago, following a lecture I gave in New Jersey, an Israeli member of the audience named Shai sought me out. He explained he had been living in the United States for 15 years, and wished he could have heard my lecture when he first arrived. It might have saved him from making all sorts of faux pas. His Israeli straightforwardness had offended his American co-workers and employees, and most likely impeded his professional advancement.

For example, Shai once explained to an employee exactly what she should do to improve her work performance. He had only the best of intentions, but the employee proceeded to cry all day long. Today he knows that his bluntness had hurt her feelings. Now he measures what he says more carefully. He is more diplomatic and tactful, and phrases his comments in a way that takes his employees and colleagues' cultural sensitivity into consideration.

Today he would present his feedback more along these lines:

- "I understand your intentions are well-meaning, but have you thought about..."

- "I agree with you on a few points, which are.... However, ..."

Shai says that using these kinds of long, drawn-out sentences fosters good dialogue, although he cynically calls them "massage words."

Comment:

Earlier, I pointed out that certain generalizations are unavoidable when considering entire cultures. Cross-cultural research is not an exact science, and obviously not all Israelis behave according to their cultural norms, just as plenty of individuals in other cultures may not always behave like most of their countrymen. In short, despite the national tendency to communicate in a curt manner, there are Israelis who behave courteously and diplomatically.

Regarding straightforwardness as a characteristic of Israeli culture, one must also take language difficulties into consideration, besides the cultural divide. Although many Israelis have a high-level knowledge of English, it is not their mother tongue. Israelis often prefer to use simple, familiar words that are easier for them to pronounce. When non-native speakers translate from their own language into English they may also tend to keep their sentences short, to minimize the possibility of making errors. The resulting vocabulary level and language structure are liable to sound unsophisticated to the native ear. Try not to mistake this for lack of intelligence or unprofessionalism.

> *Recommendation:*
>
> *Not all Israelis are aware of the differences between their culture and others. Many are oblivious to how aggressive their straightforwardness can appear to non-Israelis. When working with Israelis, try to keep this in mind, and learn to differentiate between directness in business and interpersonal sensitivity. Remember that the direct style of speech, while abrasive, can save a lot of time otherwise spent trying to figure out what is really meant beyond what is said or not said.*

Negotiations

The straightforwardness and simple communication style that are characteristic of Israeli culture don't necessarily apply to negotiations! When negotiating, both with business associates and with friends, Israelis may deviate from their usual clear-cut style. In businesses in daily life, Israelis have a strong desire to triumph, make money and prove themselves the winner in any "win-lose" situation.

Israelis might think that pulling the rope tighter will convince you to back down, and will not hesitate to do so. As a ruse they might say, "That's impossible," when in fact they know it is possible. Israelis might even say "No!" as a bluff to achieve their goal. Their combative, goal-oriented spirit stands in relative contrast to negotiated situations in the United States and Europe, where goodwill can exist between negotiators. In those places, it is more accepted that both sides should come out satisfied (win-win).

Win–Win

Win–Lose

Don't forget that despite their usual straightforwardness, Israelis are tough negotiators. Words like 'impossible' are part of the negotiations game, and a standard opening gambit.

I often get to work with new immigrants to Israel. These people have to cope with multiple difficulties at once that go far beyond a mere language barrier. At one of my workshops, a businessman who had immigrated from Hungary approached me and said that he couldn't understand why Israelis use the word 'impossible' in business when referring to things that clearly are possible. This is an excellent example of the need to understand a culture and its underlying mentality, and not just the language. When an Israeli says "That's not possible" in negotiations, it may be translated roughly as "Let's come up with a better idea/price/solution."

Remember: If Israelis challenge you, it's because they are interested in closing the deal...eventually, and with the best possible terms for themselves. They might also pursue strategic bargaining and don't always put all their cards on the table. After reaching an agreement with Israelis, make sure that you back it up unambiguously in writing, down to the smallest details.

Emotionality and Confrontationalism

In the article "Getting to Si, Ja, Oui and Da," published by the Harvard Business Review (Meyer, 2015), the author refers to the two main parameters that impact most negotiations between people from different cultures: emotional expressiveness and confrontationalism. The chart below sorts nationalities according to how confrontational and emotionally expressive they are in their negotiating style:

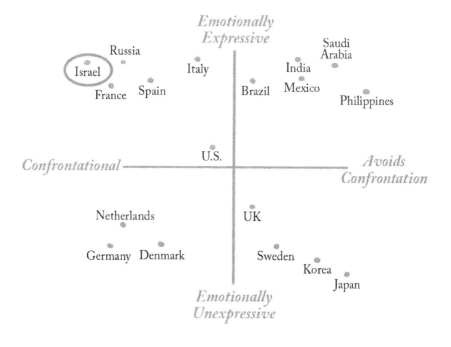

(Meyer, 2015, para. 15)

Israel's position on this chart is accurate and telling. It indicates a country that uses both an emotionally expressive and confrontational style of dialogue. In Israel people are used to debates and open disagreement, which are viewed as positive engagement even if not expressed calmly. Israelis excitedly communicate whatever they are thinking or feeling. They commonly raise their voices during negotiations as well as laugh passionately and even put a friendly arm around you, without paying any attention to the boundaries of personal space. Israeli culture encourages discussion and voicing your own opinion; someone will always ask "why?" and someone will always try to get the price down.

To forge good working relations with Israelis, you should first gauge your own place on the map. Then you can work on reducing the gap. For instance, if you're British you will probably agree that in negotiations you do not show emotions and you avoid arguments, meaning that you're in the lower right quadrant of the graph. It follows that an Israeli would have a tough time assessing when you're angry. Without cultural awareness, everyone automatically expects others to behave as they do – and when the Israeli is dissatisfied he lets it all out, verbally and non-verbally, in every direction. So there might be a situation of equal degrees of anger, but the Briton interprets the Israeli's level as much higher than it really is, while the Israeli doesn't sense the Briton's anger at all.

This kind of misunderstanding can occur with any other culture in a different quadrant than your own. The Brazilian in the upper right corner will express his anger but prefers to maintain friendly relations and not to argue about anything. The German in the lower left corner, in contrast, will continue arguing with the Israeli but will plan her points in advance, present them in a less emotional manner and use few gestures.

Interrupting

At business meetings as well as in casual conversation, Israelis often cut off the person who is talking. They can also be very associative, going off on tangents. This manner of speaking is common and can even be considered a sign of interest and enthusiasm for the subject at hand. It's just part of the way Israelis interact with others.

In most countries, especially in the West, people conduct dialogue by speaking each in turn. The listener waits until the speaker finishes before expressing his own thoughts. In Israel speech is not characterized so much by an "exchange of opinions" as by "interruptions." This can seem insulting and discourteous to non-Israelis, who tend to recoil from apparent rudeness. In the cross-cultural business world, it would be worthwhile for Israelis to listen more and talk less. On the plus side, the flexibility of the Israeli manner of speaking has a certain appeal and can potentially lead dialogues to new and interesting places.

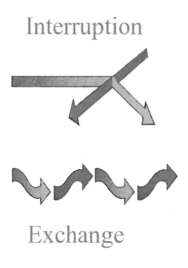

Interruption

Exchange

In Israel, "choppy" dialogue reflects enthusiasm and interest in the subject at hand and not a lack of courtesy. Understanding that this is natural in the Israeli culture may help you refrain from taking it personally. This communication style does not mean there is no room for the non-Israeli to speak. Rather, it means that during a staff meeting or conference call, you have more freedom to interrupt others. You don't have to wait to be prompted. Israelis expect to hear your opinion, too, so speak up when you have something to say.

Building Trust with Israelis

Quite a few global summits regularly take place in Israel. In just the past years Israel has hosted AWS (Amazon), IBM, Microsoft, Israel Mobile Association, Tech & Law, Edtech and many more. Such summits bring numerous businesspeople from all over the globe to Israel. Some of them are new to the Israeli market and others have been collaborating with the Israeli business world for many years.

These events also pose an opportunity for building up business relationships, which are vital in the Israeli culture. In Israel, people want to get to know you before they do business with you. Israelis make friends fairly easily, and they trust their friends. They prefer not to do business with people they don't trust. Therefore, they will take you out for dinner, ask personal questions, and invest a lot of time and energy in becoming your true friend, if possible, and getting a feel for how trustworthy you are in the process.

Erin Meyer, author of "The Culture Map" (2014), draws an important distinction in the business arena between people who trust with their head (**cognitive trust**) and those who trust with their heart (**affective trust**) (p. 168).

- Cognitive trust is built on the self-confidence you sense in another person's achievements, talents and consistency. This is trust from the head.

- Affective trust, on the other hand, develops from feelings of familiarity, sympathy or friendship. This type of trust comes from the heart.

In Israel, people build trust from their hearts and are more "relationship-based," meaning that they place the greatest importance on personal bonds rather than products, prices or any other logical, objective factor. Trust is built through sharing personal feelings and information. Besides doing business with their friends, Israelis will do business with their friends' friends. They'll do business with nice people with whom they feel they communicate well. Using emotions and intuition in business is considered completely legitimate.

For international businesspeople arriving in Israel, I would recommend:

- Sparing some time and effort for meals or social events. It's important—and it's good business—to build up long-term professional relationships.

- Using this quality time to establish personal connections and make friends with your local contacts, because it is vital to them and also bound to benefit you in more ways than one.

> *Remember:*
>
> *It's challenging to create and sustain trust, especially in the global business world. Trust is also one of the most essential qualities in any interpersonal relationship. That's why building trust, and understanding what's important to your business associates, customers, colleagues and vendors,*

> *is a farsighted, smart investment. To Israelis, open and straightforward communication is a basic element in trust relations.*

Strengthening and Softening Messages

Israelis tend to use extreme, exaggerated words like 'totally,' 'completely,' 'absolutely,' 'impossible'... Linguists call these upgraders. These emphatic words give a stronger feel to the sentence and are used to reinforce the message, e.g., "I totally disagree!" Many cultures perceive Israelis as very aggressive in how they communicate and express disagreement, particularly due to their use of upgraders along with high emotionalism, hand gestures and extreme criticism. All of this behavior could very well signify a routine, non-confrontational dialogue among Israelis.

In contrast, more indirect cultures use downgraders—phrases like 'kind of,' 'a little,' 'maybe'—to soften messages. These words are used especially when giving negative feedback or other criticism. For instance, when a British manager gently mentions in a one-on-one conversation that "I suggest you do something differently," most Israelis would be sure this literally is a mere suggestion and probably decide not to do it! The British manager, however, actually meant: "Make some changes right away." Israelis have difficulty picking up on this polite form of speech and may have trouble understanding the precise intention and meaning.

Translation Guide

What downgraders say	What downgraders mean	What Israelis understand
Very interesting.	Not at all interesting.	He loves it.
That is an original point of view.	Wow – bad idea.	Well, we are the startup nation! Original ideas are my specialty. I'm so happy he likes the idea. ☺
Please think about that some more.	Simply unacceptable.	The direction is good and I need to keep developing it.
Perhaps you could think about...	This is an order.	I'll think about his suggestion, then I'll do what I decide is right.
I was a bit disappointed that...	I am very upset.	No big deal, he'll get over it.

(Based on a model by Ripmeester, in Rottier, Ripmeester & Bush, 2011)

My recommendation to Israelis working with cultures that use downgraders is to ignore the soft words surrounding a message. That will help you get the right idea. Also, in order not to be perceived as so aggressive I recommend that Israelis make a concerted effort to remove exaggerated words like "totally" or "completely." They can also soften their own messages by adding some positive and appreciative comments to people from other cultures.

Communication across cultures is like dancing the tango: two steps forward and one step back. That's why I recommend that Israelis "take a step back" and say, "We can come up with a better idea" instead of "That's a terrible idea." Saying (and thinking) along the lines of "There's been a slight misunderstanding," rather than "You've completely missed the point!" will also greatly improve the communication.

I   Informal

S   Straightforward

R   Risk-Taking

A   Ambitious

E   Entrepreneurial

L   Loud

I   Improvisational

Risk-Taking + Ambitious = Entrepreneurial

The next three characteristics are treated as one unit, since I consider the combination of **risk-taking** and **ambition** to jointly create the characteristic of **entrepreneurialism**, forming an integral part of it.

Entrepreneurial is a mindset, not a business model.

Being entrepreneurial means:

- Knowing an industry inside out and being able to exploit that knowledge to create new opportunities.

- Celebrating failures as learning and growing experiences.

- Thinking differently and expecting the unexpected.

- Doing something that hasn't been done before to achieve a desirable goal or outcome.

- Having the gut wisdom to take a risk because you just can't do more of the same.

An entrepreneur is an individual with the capability and ambition to successfully create something new, as well as the willingness to take risks to achieve it.

The Entrepreneurial Spirit

> *The well-known Biblical story of David and Goliath (I Samuel 17-18) may help us better understand the success of Israeli entrepreneurs. It is a story of risk-taking, audacity and self-confidence. When King David was a youth, the Philistines were fighting the Israelites. Goliath was the Philistines' best warrior. Young David stepped up to fight him with only an improvised slingshot and raw courage. He faced the unknown and won. Every Israeli child learns this story and its lessons about bravery and initiative. It has helped shape each generation and of course is relevant to Israeli business culture.*

Israelis are driven to prove their worth. They may have been influenced by the history of their country, which had to fight and defeat many enemies to achieve independence. Entrepreneurs have grown up with the legacy of their parents and grandparents, who dared or were forced to leave their comfortable homes and families in Christian and Muslim countries and come to build the new country of Israel. They are spurred on by the motto: **Think more, try harder and be prepared to dare**.

In 2010 the Israeli newspaper "Globes" published an article (Peretz, 2010) in which eight leading Israeli entrepreneurs were asked what they think are the main characteristics of the successful Israeli entrepreneur.

The following unique personality characteristics were identified:

- Courage

- Sophistication

- Innovativeness

- Creativity

- Perseverance

In June 2018, Israel's 70th anniversary was celebrated in Los Angeles. Billy Crystal was one of the many stars who arrived for the LA event. Billy is an American-Jewish actor, producer, and television host. He has also hosted the Academy Awards nine times. This is how he summarized Israel (qtd in Hartog, 2018):

> *"If a nation can be built out of desert sand, if a homeland can be created out of the worst tragedy of human history, if a democracy can thrive in a region that has none, then anything and everything is possible. And that is Israel. Everything is possible."*

Successful Israeli Entrepreneurs

There are scores of successful entrepreneurs in Israel. Following are summaries of some of the most prominent ones:

The Founding Generation:

(Photo: LeWeb, 2011)

<u>**Yossi Vardi**</u> has occupied senior managerial positions since a very young age. He came into public awareness when he helped his son Arik build and sell the company Mirabilis, which had previously developed the ICQ instant messaging software, to the Internet giant AOL in 1998. ICQ's dramatic exit story (which eventually became the inspiration for the Israeli TV series "Mesudarim") became well known because of Vardi's unique reaction to the takeover bid from AOL and its original purchase offer of 225 million dollars. Vardi rejected the offer, a move strongly opposed by his partners. Only after he subsequently succeeded in selling the company for 407 million dollars did the investors realize that Vardi was nothing less than a business genius. Since then, he has managed to sell more than ten start-up companies, and received an honorary doctorate degree from Technion University. Vardi encourages entrepreneurship and innovation at conferences in Israel and around the world.

"If you look on a timeline of a company, you see that in the beginning you have to come up with an idea and to be willing to take risk. You have to grow fast, and to think fast, and you have to do this usually in small teams."

– Yossi Vardi (Berman, 2013)

Shai Agassi's entrepreneurial aspirations began early on. Upon his discharge from the Israeli army, he and his father started his first programming company, Top Tier (originally called Quicksoft Development), which he sold to SAP for 400 million dollars in 2001. Agassi became the president of the Product & Technology Group at SAP. A few years ago he left this senior position and started a new company called Better Place. His vision was to create a revolution in the car industry by manufacturing electric cars. Unfortunately for him, the company went bankrupt, but it is impossible not to admire his vision and efforts.

Noam Lanir suffers from severe Attention Deficit Disorder. He barely finished high school. He cannot sit through business meetings or keep to a regular work schedule. Nonetheless, Lanir is one of the most successful entrepreneurs in Israel. He began his career in 1990 as a public relations advisor for Tel Aviv nightclubs. In a radical shift, he and a partner subsequently established Empire Online in 1998, a company which marketed gambling websites. In 2005, the company was valued at one billion dollars. Today he is the controlling shareholder and CEO of the Livermore Investment Group, formerly known as Empire

Online, and Chairman of the Board of Directors of Babylon, the world leader in online translations. Lanir is also the founder of Life Tree Marketing, a company that markets the medical services of Israeli hospitals to residents of the Commonwealth of Independent States.

Gil Shwed began learning computer programming at age 13 and continued to develop his skills while in high school. He studied Computer Science at the Hebrew University before serving in the army, in the elite intelligence unit 8200. After his discharge, Gil and two partners founded Checkpoint in 1993, which became one of the largest data protection companies in the world. Gil remains the CEO of Checkpoint to this day. In 2010 he was named Israeli Entrepreneur of the Year by Ernst and Young. In 2014, Globes, one of Israel's largest financial outlets, honored Shwed as their "Person of the Year." In 2015, he ranked 12th richest Israeli in TheMarker magazine (Avriel, 2015). And in 2018, Shwed received the first-ever Israel Prize in Technology.

The New Generation:

Uri Levine is one of the most productive, tireless businessmen today and an angel investor in technology-based companies. He is a cofounder and the chairman of FeeX, which targets the problem of hidden charges in financial services. His greatest business success has been cofounding and selling Waze, the mapping and navigation app that enables users to avoid traffic jams, which was acquired by Google in 2013 for over one billion dollars. Nowadays, he combines his business activities with investing in startups and helping people develop their own innovative projects, such as Moovit, Engie and Fairfly.

Yaron Galai cofounded Outbrain in 2006 and has served as its CEO ever since. Outbrain is an online advertiser specializing in presenting sponsored website links. Its promoted articles, videos, blogs and many other links are found on more than 35,000 websites, serve over 250 billion recommendations and receive 15 billion page views per month.

Adam Neumann cofounded, with Miguel McKelvey, the communal work space giant WeWork in 2010. The company, under CEO Neumann, designs and builds physical and virtual shared spaces and office services for entrepreneurs and companies, renting out offices in over 40 cities around the world. It has raised over $2.5 billion from investors like Goldman Sachs and Softbank, and its latest valuation was $21 billion.

Avishai Avrahami is an experienced technology entrepreneur who has grown Wix.com from a startup in 2006 to the world's leading do-it-yourself web publishing platform. Avishai and his co-founders developed Wix out of frustration with the complexities of website creation. Since then, they've helped tens of millions of users with no development skills craft attractive, professional websites. In 2014 Wix also launched Wix Hotels, a booking system for hotels, B&Bs and vacation rentals that use Wix websites. This was followed in 2015 by Wix Music, a platform for independent musicians to market and sell their music, and by Wix Restaurants in 2016.

Dave (Shahar) Waiser is a cofounder and the CEO of the ridesharing company Gett (previously known as GetTaxi). Waiser came up with the idea in 2009 during a thirty-minute wait for a taxi to the airport in Palo Alto, California. GetTaxi's beta version started operating in Tel Aviv two years later, in 2011. Gett is the go-to taxi app supported by thousands of cabbies in more than 100 cities around the world. Customers can order a taxi or courier either through the company website or by using its GPS-based smartphone app. Gett raised $640 million in venture funding, including $300 million from Volkswagen Group, and in 2016 was selected by Forbes as one of the 15 fastest growing companies.

> *In Israel, being a leader means having chutzpah (audacity), ambition and curiosity. Motivated people begin the race for success while serving in the IDF. The army teaches them to be innovative, take charge of developments and assume responsibility for the consequences. This early, challenging starting point turns them into fighters and leaders at a young age, and they bring these same qualities to their work as entrepreneurs.*

Dan Senor and Saul Singer try to explain the relatively huge number of successful entrepreneurs in minuscule Israel in their book "Start-up Nation" (2009). They found that Israel, relatively small and steeped in so many existential difficulties, has more startup companies than other, much larger and much more stable countries with many more resources. They conclude that the challenges encountered in Israel serve as catalysts, pushing Israelis to succeed.

Difficulty-Driven Success

Among the world's leading economies, Israel is ranked second in the category of business growth environments. Grant Thornton, the company that conducts research for the GDI – Global Dynamism Index, wrote: "Did you know, for example, that Israel has the highest concentration of hi-tech companies in the world outside of Silicon Valley? Or that Israel has more scientists and technicians per capita than any other economy?" (Halperin, 2013).

Objectively speaking, Israel does not have it easy. The World Bank report "Doing Business" (2016) ranks Israel in 52nd place worldwide out of 190 countries regarding the general ease of conducting all aspects of business, far behind the U.S. (8th), New Zealand (1st), Denmark (3rd) and Britain (7th). The World Bank also ranks Israel 98th in the paying taxes indicator and 89th in contract enforcement.

Difficult circumstances are ingrained and constant in Israeli life. As mentioned earlier, Israel is a tiny country surrounded by enemies. Israeli businesspeople know that the local market share is limited. Moreover, unlike in Europe, travelling to neighboring states to do business is not an option. So, from childhood on we are taught to think big, to understand the paramount value of English as a second language, and to create products that target the global market.

Sure, it might be nice if we could lead calmer lives like in Switzerland or New Zealand, but here in the State of Israel, grappling with our many challenges propels us forward to success. Many individuals living in little Israel have almost infinite ambition and are prepared to take risks. This combination leads to triumphant coping with the difficulties along the way and becoming the cream of the crop in their fields. On a practical level, when you encounter an obstacle, you must delve into the essence of the reality you're facing as well as the essence and feasibility of your own desires. **When you grow up constantly having to sink or swim, you learn to swim really well.**

Dr. Amit Goffer, founder of the ReWalk robotics company, had to deal not only with the difficulties involved in setting up a new company in Israel but also with the personal tragedy that rendered him a quadriplegic and spurred him to develop the ReWalk wearable exoskeleton.

One day in 1997, Dr. Goffer – an electronics engineer and medical equipment entrepreneur, set out for his first and last ever ride on an ATV (All Terrain Vehicle). The vehicle was faulty and slammed into a tree trunk, breaking Dr. Goffer's neck and leaving him paralyzed. His condition inspired him to work relentlessly, day and night, trying to find a way to avoid being stuck in a wheelchair for the rest of his life.

After conceiving the product and learning there were over a million quadriplegics in the Western world who could potentially benefit from the ReWalk wearable exoskeleton, he got the new company up and running, so to speak. Unfortunately, so far Dr. Goffer has personally been unable to take advantage of the product he developed, but ReWalk is providing hope and improving lives for hundreds of disabled persons the world over. In 2015, the U.S. Department of Veterans Affairs purchased ReWalk personal exoskeleton systems for all qualifying veterans across the United States.

Bruce Lee famously once said, "To hell with the circumstances, I create opportunities!" And that can describe the Israeli culture as well: Israelis create opportunities; they exit the bubble of difficulty and enter the creative world, where they take chances and don't give up. Israelis created the Smart Dripper to address the matter of irrigation in a semi-arid climate. They developed the Iron Dome system in response to incessant missile attacks on Israeli civilians. Israelis developed the Waze navigation app due to the endless traffic jams in the crowded little country. They take lemons and make million-dollar, world-changing lemonade...

> *Israelis exhibit a tendency to criticize others. Someone is always on hand to pass judgment or attribute success to pure luck. Confident, successful entrepreneurs are not deterred by the envy of others. The tough life in Israel, including army experience, usually gives Israelis thick skins, and good entrepreneurs do not let naysayers hold them back. More than that, successful entrepreneurial business figures must be able to make difficult and intuitive decisions. They have an overall vision and possess the ability, against all odds, to turn their vision into reality. The road to success is not easy, and entrepreneurs must always be optimistic. They must be able to push aside the doubts and negativism of their more conservative colleagues.*

Israel is one of the world leaders not only in high-tech but innumerous other realms as well, such as physics, medicine, economy, security, biotechnology and agriculture. For example, environmental necessity has led to cutting edge developments. A lack of natural resources, extreme heat for much of the year and a shortage of water necessitated the development of "smart," modern agriculture. Agricultural entrepreneurs have devised many ways to increase production on limited tracts of land. Developments in Israeli agriculture have been disseminated to farmers in many other areas of the world, which in turn has furthered the efforts to cope with burgeoning populations. The countless success stories in this field include advancements in drip irrigation and the development of new types of seedlings for decorative plants, herbs, olive trees, date palms, algae oil, etc.

The Positive Attitude Toward Failure in the Culture of Israeli Innovation

Business practices and behavior in any culture is largely connected to the cultural mindset in general. Israeli society has a positive attitude toward failure; Israelis see a person who has failed as someone who has tried. In business, Israelis know that entrepreneurs learn and gain from past unsuccessful experiences on the road to eventual success.

As an Israeli who researches her own culture, I am used to hearing Israeli businesspeople speak freely about both their failures and their successes in the global business world. I once interviewed an NYU student who had been living in Israel for eight months as part of his NYU Tel Aviv program. When I asked about his most enriching experience in terms of the cultural gap, he said: "During my stay in Israel, I have met a few entrepreneurs, and I reached the conclusion that in the Israeli innovation culture, failure is considered a positive thing. That is quite different from other cultures, such as China, because in other cultures people hide their failures. In Israel I've learned that the real key to success is to be proud of failure, as it is a good opportunity to learn from experience."

In such a risky environment, where only a small percentage of start-up companies "make it," entrepreneurs must hold on to optimism. A major part of optimism is embracing your mistakes and failed attempts. Entrepreneurs are always looking for excitement and are willing to take chances. This kind of risk acceptance is another reason why Israel has so many successful startup companies.

Entrepreneurs believe that no product can come to life risk-free. True innovation requires a trial-and-error process, so taking a calculated risk is an essential part of the process. And failure is an opportunity for learning; not a cause for embarrassment or something to be concealed, but quite the contrary.

> **"Israeli entrepreneurs shoot very high. Sometimes that's good and sometimes that's bad. But whichever, success or failure, it is always on a large scale."**
>
> *– Bruno Landsberg, founder of the Sano manufacturing company*
> *(Peretz, 2010)*

5 Facts That Have Shaped Israelis as Entrepreneurs

1. Objective circumstances

From Israel's very first day as a new country in its ancestral land, Israelis have understood that this is a place where absolutely everything must be fought for. Nothing is comfortable or certain, and not even their existence may be taken for granted.

2. High-power "melting pot"

Israel ingathered not only persecuted refugees but also people of strong faith and ambition. It became a melting pot of brave souls. To this day, optimistic, idealistic, creative new immigrants continue to arrive from North America and from France and the rest of Europe.

3. Military service

Israel defends its security with the help of almost all its citizens. The Israel Defense Forces are a people's army, with mandatory conscription for both men and women. Early on, it became a mission-oriented society in which military values spill over into civilian life. Its cities and towns are all on the front line; its soldiers are literally protecting their families and homes. They fight responsibly and bravely, and then bring that same mentality into the professional and business realms, as well as everyday living.

4. Acceptance of failure

In Asian cultures there is a great fear of failing. Failure is a source of shame in front of friends and family as well as colleagues. In Israel, businesspeople who have failed say so openly and flippantly, even proudly. As said above, failing is part of their personal lore about gaining experience and learning how to properly manage subsequent endeavors. Already in elementary school, teachers encourage schoolchildren to dare and attempt new challenges. The emphasis is on trying and not giving up.

> "Behind every journey of success there is a history of failure."
>
> *– Waze cofounder Uri Levine (Alba, 2016)*

5. Ecosystem

An entrepreneur needs a supportive environment, such as that which evolved in Israel, starting with entrepreneurs who "made it" and then became "angels" (investors using private capital) and mentors for the next generation, and up through government support via the Israeli Innovation Authority (formerly the Office of the Chief Scientist).

Israelis live and breathe innovation. Israel has over 90 accelerators, the most well-known being Microsoft Ventures, IBM Alpha Zone and 8200 EISP. Just in the center of the country are more than 50 co-working spaces and shared hubs, such as WeWork, SOSA, Mindspace and many, many more.

Giant corporations have long since opened their own innovation and R&D centers in Israel, e.g., IBM, Ebay, HP, AT&T. The digital mapping service Here, owned by the major German carmakers Audi, BMW, and Daimler-Mercedes, is also currently establishing an innovation center in Israel as well.

Now the question is: How can Israel take a step forward from being the "Start-up Nation" to becoming an international business powerhouse nation?

I don't have an answer to that question. But I can certainly see a change in the outlook of many young managers in Israel. They're paying more attention to detail and doing some long-term strategic planning. These are new in Israel! These trailblazers are still dreaming big and forging ahead like the old generation, but now they're also looking sideways to learn some business savvy from other, more established superpowers.

A Closer Look: Entrepreneurial Qualities

The Connection Between MVP and the Israeli Innovation Culture

In today's startup world, people talk about a term called MVP: Minimum Viable Product. The idea behind it is to quickly validate your startup at an early stage: check how the market reacts to your product, validate customer needs and assess other parameters before spending unnecessary time and money on developing the product.

In a blog published by David Tsalani (2014), I found a great example, taken from the Spotify product development team, which demonstrates the MVP way of thinking:

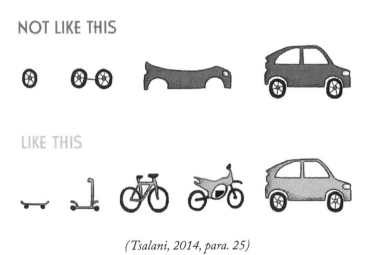

(*Tsalani, 2014, para. 25*)

"If you want to sell a car (your successful end product) to your customer for the X price, a lot of times a badly designed MVP/landing page might look a lot like a wheel (see picture). Instead of creating a wheel (incomplete MVP), think of something that would provide customers with the complete experience of getting from A to B faster than walking. A skateboard might be a very simplified solution to that and it requires a lot of manual power, but it is that complete experience and a faster way to get to B. And, of course, it is much cheaper and faster to build compared to the car."

After reading the blog and the example mentioned above, it became clear to me that the MVP approach can also explain the Israeli innovation culture. Israelis will not invent the next Mercedes, but they will build some good-enough other vehicle or product that will be ready much quicker and for much cheaper. That's what counts in today's volatile technological world: being fast, smart and, of course, useful.

The qualities of entrepreneurship and innovativeness are an inseparable part of Israelis' culture. They think strategically for the short term, improvise, take risks, don't waste time going into the small details, and are practical and adaptable to changes along the way. In my viewpoint, based on my experience in working with and researching global Israeli-owned companies, the underlying idea of the term MVP expresses precisely who we are in the Israeli culture.

A Prophetic Message from a Founding Father

Yitzhak Navon, the fifth president of the State of Israel, was a modest man, and an educator with strong values and a great love of humanity. He passed away on November 6, 2015. Six years before he died at age 88, the former president decided to sit in front of a video camera and speak for almost an hour about his past, and mainly to convey his message for the future. Navon, who was from the generation of Israel's founding fathers, is the first Israeli politician and educator to have left a video will, and did so with a message of progress and technology, and their extreme importance.

(Photo: Wierzba, 2010)

In the early years after the proclamation of the State, Navon headed the office of Israel's first Prime Minister, David Ben-Gurion. When asked in the video interview about Ben-Gurion's worldview, Navon replied that it could be summed up in this statement of Ben-Gurion's:

"We can never compete with our rivals, who are now enemies, not in wealth, assets, oil or minerals, but only in quality, and moral, scientific, and technological superiority. And the condition for Israel's existence is dependent on quality, on the face of the society we represent. They'll also always have more tanks and planes and people, but scientific-technological superiority will aid us in our hour of need."

(Ben-Gurion qtd in Navon, 2009, in Sherki, 2015)

It is remarkable to realize that back in the 1950s, just a few years after the establishment of the State in 1948, the fledgling nation's first leader already knew that Israel would enjoy a scientific and technological advantage. It's as if he was marking out the path of who Israel is today – a small, young country that has been labeled "the startup nation."

I Informal

S Straightforward

R Risk-Taking

A Ambitious

E Entrepreneurial

L Loud

I Improvisational

Loud

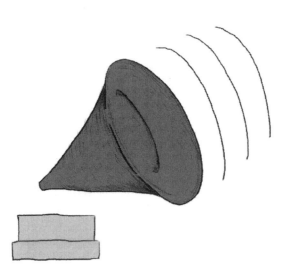

The word "loud" is quite fitting for the Israeli communication style. It can imply:

- High volume and offensive tone

- Emotional temperament

- "Noisy" body language, including much use of the hands and arms

- More emphasis on talking; less on listening

- Intensity in all areas of life

First-time visitors to Israel tell of sensing "busy noise" everywhere. It comes from the multitudes of families walking the streets, customers sitting at outdoor café tables, crowded roads and packed supermarkets. Visitors experience a lack of personal space, reflected in constant touching and straightforward questioning. There are no straight lines, and when waiting in banks, on the road or in public places, one's place must be carefully guarded. All this makes for an impression of "noise" and disorder.

Anecdote:

To examine how non-Israelis perceive Israeli colleagues, I have interviewed nearly one hundred people from different cultures who have had some form of contact with Israeli business culture. Alan is an American who has worked for some years as a senior executive in a global Israeli company. When we met, he emotionally told me about the culture shock he experienced while still working at a small American startup that was being acquired by a large Israeli company.

Prior to his first encounter with Israel, his only exposure to the country was through frightening CNN news broadcasts. Alan came to Israel for a meeting concerning the Israeli company's intention to acquire the American firm. He expressed how surprised and impressed he was by the modern international Israeli airport, the vibrant leisure time culture, the delicious food, the recreational mood on the Tel Aviv beach and the elegant Israeli headquarter offices.

The meeting started off in a pleasant atmosphere, including food and drink, warm small talk and smiles. However, the two Israeli executives present at the meeting fairly quickly began arguing loudly about several critical points in the contract. They seemed angry and switched to Hebrew. Of course Alan could not understand, but he gathered from the loud tones, rapid hand movements and contorted facial expressions that there were some major obstacles to closing the deal. He was sure it had fallen through.

To his great surprise, at the end of the meeting the Israeli men put their hands on each other's shoulders and said, smiling, "So, what are we having for lunch?" For Alan, this was a shock. How could they go on as though nothing was wrong after raising their voices in such apparent anger? The punch line is that the agreement was finally approved after lunch, and Alan has been working in the merged Israeli company ever since. These days, he doesn't get so upset about what he perceived back then as discourteous and disruptive behavior. **He claims to have learned that Israelis simply need to be heard.**

Recommendation:

Allow Israelis to say what they want to, and as loud as they need to. It may not always be easy to hear, but accepting their style of speaking without getting offended or overly distracted by it will help both sides reach optimal business results more smoothly and quickly.

Social Distance

Loudness seems to be connected to social boundaries in general. Anthropologist Edward T. Hall has written about the anthropology of space (1966). He notes that in different countries in the Western world, commonly understood interpersonal distances are maintained between people who feel close to each other. He calls this "intimate space," defining it as a distance of about 46 cm (18"). This distance is usually observed between family members, close friends, doctors and patients.

In contrast, a greater interpersonal distance of between 46 cm (18") and 1.2 m (4') is generally maintained between people in a business meeting, for example, or strangers making small talk.

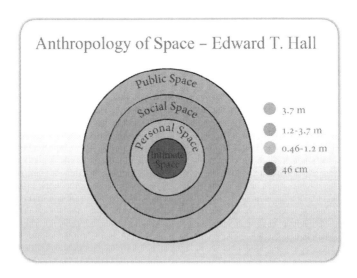

(Based on Hall, 1966, pp. 119-125)

In Israel, many people cross these boundaries. Even when they don't know you very well, they may stand very close while speaking to you. They might put a hand on your shoulder, even if you are a stranger.

In the cross-cultural workshops that I lead, I introduce an exercise that effectively demonstrates these different interpersonal distances. I sit down and ask a non-Israeli to bring his chair closer and closer to mine until he begins to feel uncomfortable. Most participants will stop at least 46 cm (18") away from me. Then I ask an Israeli to do the same thing. He comes closer and closer...and then even closer than 46 cm (18")...until it becomes uncomfortable for **me**, and in the end **I** ask **him** to stop.

In addition, a lack of separation between personal and business life is reflected in many ways in Israel. Israelis tend to form close friendships at work. During school vacations, they may bring their children to the workplace. They may speak to family members on the phone while at work. But, on the flip side, they often bring work home, where they put in long extra hours. And they may contact colleagues during evening hours much more often than non-Israelis would ever do.

Attitudes Towards Time

Different cultures also have different attitudes towards time. In Switzerland, for example, all activity functions according to relatively fixed schedules. Universally, when things are going precisely according to plan, they are "running like a Swiss clock." To an Israeli, this may appear enviable but also rigid. In Switzerland, early is on time, and on time is late. Israelis, however, often run behind schedule, and seem to be more comfortable when the attitude towards time is more flexible.

Edward T. Hall's book "The Silent Language" (1959) categorizes these two different cultural attitudes towards time as **monochronic culture** and **polychronic culture**. In monochronic cultures (such as the United States, Germany, Switzerland and Scandinavia), time is seen as a resource that must be harnessed with the help of fixed schedules and regular time periods. Every unit of time is devoted to carrying out one task alone. In contrast, in polychronic cultures (such as Israel, France, Italy, Greece and Mexico), many activities can be carried out simultaneously. There is less need to stick to a fixed schedule.

(Photo: Rawpixel.com, n.d.)

These different ways of relating to time have many ramifications for styles of work. Israel, as a polychronic culture, enables a work style that:

- Allows for coping with more than one task at a time.

- Views timetables as a goal but not necessarily the main one.

- Allows for the exchange and flow of much, and sometimes varied, information.

- Enables a relatively flexible attitude towards starting times.

- Views interruptions as acceptable.

- Understands that people come before tasks.

- Permits employees to work flexible hours.

- Accepts that meetings may not follow the planned structure.

- Supports an employee wearing several different hats.

- Accepts responding to phone calls and sending or receiving emails during meetings.

As part of my ongoing research on Israeli culture, I interview workers at different levels in international organizations who have contact with Israelis. One such interview was with Sara, a senior executive assistant. Sara, who is in her 70s, has vast experience working with Israelis. Her family came from Europe, and it was hard for her to get used to the Israeli business culture. She receives many emails from administrative assistants in the organization, and sometimes the content of Israeli email is labeled URGENT. In Western culture, particularly in North America and Europe, the word "urgent" comes across loud and clear. It insists on giving the issue top priority, with pressing time constraints.

In Israeli business culture, however, the word may have other meanings. It can mean that the matter is simply important. It may have been inserted just to gain the reader's attention. Other Israelis can sense whether URGENT conveys that the matter is truly urgent or something less immediate, but non-Israelis understandably may get confused.

Such a cultural difference in how a word is perceived may lead to a situation of "the boy who cried wolf." The first time a non-Israeli receives a request marked URGENT from an Israeli, he may relate to it with haste. The second and third times, he may still deal with it quickly, putting other matters aside. Eventually he comes to understand the use of the word URGENT in its proper cultural perspective, and doesn't necessarily drop everything else in order to handle the matter, or even to read the email as quickly as he would have done otherwise.

Recommendation for Non-Israelis:

Communication in heterogeneous groups sometimes requires asking additional questions. Check whether the matter really is urgent rather than just important by asking, for example: How urgent is this? What's the actual deadline for getting the task done?

To the Israelis among you who are reading this book, my recommendation is to use the word URGENT only when the subject is truly time-critical.

Cultural Argumentativeness

The Israeli inclination for debate may be related to Judaism. The Jewish religion, and therefore Israeli culture as well, encourages discussion and argument. In Israel we have the amusing expression: "Two Jews – three opinions."

> "The Jews' greatest contribution to history is dissatisfaction!"
>
> – Shimon Peres, President of the State of Israel 2007-2014
> (Haaretz, 2016)

In most business meetings in Israel, one gets the sense that arguments are a vital component of the decision-making process. More often than not, argument and conflict during meetings simply enable opinions to be expressed, creating healthy competition or support and identification. Seldom do they threaten the participants' social and professional relationships.

I recently read an interesting article about Israeli slang expressions and their amusing translations into English (Yanay, 2016). Here are two examples from the article:

'SOF HADERECH' – Literally means 'end of the road' but used to describe something awesome. Like, 'that party was end of the road.'

'AL HA'PANIM' – Translates to 'on the face.' Used to describe when something was really awful. "The food tonight was on my face," meaning 'very bad.'

The article is nicely written and provides a peek into Israeli culture and its spoken slang. But more than the content, what really interested me this time were the many comments by readers, 68 of them by the time I read it. Most of the comments were from Israelis and literally all of them were arguments about the origins, meanings and translations of the slang terms.

Almost every detail in the article was put on the Internet pulpit of public debate. That's exactly what happens in our daily lives in the public and business arena in Israel.

In New Zealand culture, just for a contrasting example, people aim for equality and tranquility, sharing and consensus. Accordingly, at a New Zealand business meeting, participants conduct themselves quietly. A protocol is kept, and no loud opposition or arguments are expressed. Writing things down is their way of caring for the process. Israelis, on the other hand, show how much they care by making themselves heard.

In today's Israeli business culture, argument and discussion take place directly and sometimes bluntly, in high tones and aggressive body language, such as leaning forward, standing, making hand gestures, etc. Is argument a type of Israeli directness, a need for conflict and emotional expression, or just an element of Jewish tradition?

It's hard to say. But in any case, it exists, also in the business environment. And yes, there is a definite need to be heard! Argument stimulates the entire process, emotional sharing and thinking outside the box, leading to surprisingly successful business results. **Most importantly, those of you from other cultures should remember that it is an Israeli characteristic and certainly not directed at you personally.**

A Closer Look: The Nuances of Loudness

The Power of Listening

Communication is not just about speaking but also listening. Communicating well across different cultures involves listening closely enough to not only hear the words but also be aware of the speaker's true meaning. Even when everyone is using the same language, and most certainly in English-speaking cultures, much is happening below the surface, meaning that the volume of the conversation, how things are phrased, which things are left unsaid and even the way body gestures are incorporated, all bear unique significance in different cultures.

Communication is a two-way process, involving both the communicative skills of the speaker and the listening skills of the interlocutor. Richard D. Lewis has pointed out in "When Cultures Collide" (2006) that different cultures have different communication styles and different listening habits. Germans listen for information. People from the UK listen politely, add some smiles and nods, and only occasionally interrupt for clarification. Americans listen in spurts, while people in Sweden cooperate and even whisper some feedback. In Finland there are no interruptions and in Japan listeners never disrupt the speaker's flow.

Israelis are impatient and their eagerness to voice their own opinions makes them poor listeners. However, just because Israelis consider their straightforwardness a virtue doesn't mean everyone else is the same, or that Israelis needn't be sensitive to others' cultural subtleties.

Israelis, please remember the old adage:

God gave us two ears and one mouth, which we should use accordingly by listening more and speaking less, most especially across cultures.

Heder Vahetzi App as a Metaphor for Israeli Business Culture

The mobile app "Heder Vahetzi" (One and a Half Rooms), based on an animated segment of the satirical Israeli entertainment show "Eretz Nehederet" (A Wonderful Country), provides a marvelous example of Israeli intensity and constant change.

The segment and the app deal with the life of a young bachelor, Shuli, and interaction with objects in his home. The app targets Hebrew-speaking players and within a short time had already been downloaded by 800,000 users, making it a huge success for a country with only 8.5 million residents.

The app contains a number of stages that the player has to get through quickly. The player is asked to help Shuli, a single Tel-Avivian, with various tasks. These include waking up Shuli on time, while his alarm clock is hidden behind a pigeon; guiding the robotic cleaner to avoid vacuuming broken glass; catching pieces of toast flying out of the toaster; remembering the order of the products on the refrigerator shelf; and getting through 10 other fast stages that are both cool and funny.

"Wake up Shuli at 7:00 a.m."
(Heder Vahetzi screenshot)

You get three tries (represented by hearts) in each round of the game. Every time you pass or fail a stage, the hearts react in a chorus, using slang words, humor and sounds taken from popular Israeli culture. For instance, when you successfully complete a task, the chorus sings out phrases meaning things like "You stud," "What a star" and "You've got the genes of a scientist"... And when you fail: "What a loser," "I expected more from you" and "Let's do this again but better"...

Most leading apps, such as Temple Run (a 3D game developed by Imangi Studios in Washington) or King's Candy Crush, incorporate gamification mechanisms that allow the player to learn the rules of the game while using the app and gradually advancing from easy to more challenging stages. In the Israeli app Heder Vahetzi, there's really only one stage, without any easy stages leading into it. No preparation or learning process takes place or is even possible. Everything is basically intense and fast from the get-go. You just jump in and immediately have to perform the tasks. Other surprising stages come along the way, with amusing figures who try to make your life harder.

The Heder Vahetzi app aptly represents the fast, loud Israeli society and business culture. In the business realm, however, people from other cultures find this Israeli conduct less amusing and sometimes also unprofessional. At a business meeting with Israelis, people tend to jump around from one subject to another, ask a lot of questions and cut each other off in mid-sentence. Some Israelis will suddenly exit and reenter the room during a meeting; some will go off for a planned five-minute break and come back after 15 minutes or more. Sentences in Hebrew will be interjected here and there before reverting to English.

In Israel, anything goes... you have to expect the unexpected.

I Informal
S Straightforward
R Risk-Taking
A Ambitious
E Entrepreneurial
L Loud
I Improvisational

Improvisational

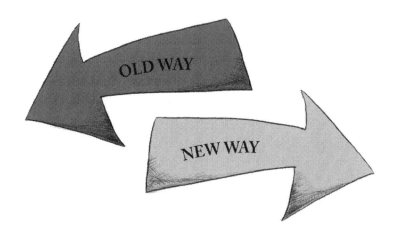

Improvisation is related to creativity in all realms.

The culture of improvisation in Israel supports "thinking outside the box." This means not just going along with an existing plan but continually thinking, initiating and changing until the desired goal is reached, especially in accordance with changes and challenges that arise along the way.

"Insanity is doing the same thing over and over again and expecting different results."

– Albert Einstein

Anecdote:

5min.com is an example of an Israeli company that thought "outside the box." Back in 2007, it was founded by Ran Harnevo, Hanan Lashover and Tal Simantov as a social platform for sharing "how to" videos. Users immediately started utilizing the website to share DIY (Do it Yourself) videos, unintentionally placing the young company in competition with leading DIY and knowledge sites such as answers.com. Having to deal with the new situation, and recognizing the advantages of their own technology, the 5min.com team decided to change their strategy. They refashioned their site as a "video anywhere" platform that supported other DIY/knowledge websites, thereby turning their competitors into customers.

Thinking outside the box and adjusting their strategy was a great move for 5min.com, which became a worldwide leading video syndication platform. In 2010, the company was acquired by AOL for $65 million, while Harnevo become the AOL Video Division president, Simantov the division CMO and Lashover the CEO of AOL Israel.

We'll Cross That Bridge When We Come to It

Most local and international companies understand the strategic importance of long-term planning and careful attention to detail. Yet there is often a discrepancy in the way international companies and Israeli companies view these matters. In Israel the difficult day-to-day reality, owing to the tense security and political situation in the Middle East, can lead to existential uncertainty and, in business life, contribute to the improvisational atmosphere and lack of careful, long-term planning.

Israeli businesspeople can identify general business trends and visions, but tend to minimize the importance of planning ahead. They maintain certain values and goals, but everything is open to change along the way. People in Israel often say, in business as in daily life, "We'll cross that bridge when we come to it," and "Don't worry, everything will work out fine."

(Photo: Lightspring, n.d.)

I witnessed an excellent example of cultural differences among various nationalities at a recent conference I attended in London. Companies presented their products and services at the event, but devoted hardly any time to product features and capabilities. Their presentations focused mainly on the company's vision and the value it brings to their customers. The Europeans, Americans and Asians present were very impressed and responded favorably to the precise statements about company philosophy. In contrast, the Israelis behaved as if nothing of interest had been said. They just wanted to hear about the latest product features and enhancements in more detail. I attribute this to Israelis' brass-tacks approach and their need for practical facts and actions to focus and elaborate on, rather than the underlying long-term rationale, because who knows what tomorrow will bring?

"Yihyeh Beseder"

Danny Sanderson is an Israel guitarist, singer, musician, composer and producer. Formerly a member of the classic Israeli band Kaveret, he is considered one of the fathers of Israeli rock music. Here are the lyrics of a song he composed that reflects the Israeli attitude towards improvisation:

The Unknown
©All rights reserved to Danny Sanderson and ACUM

We're going to the unknown,
To the unknown
To the unknown
We're going to who knows where

Whether it's good or bad
In the unknown.
Without knowing our fate
Or what will be
Everyone guesses what's ahead
There in the unknown
Going to the unknown...

(Unofficial translation from Hebrew)

A song like this, which nearly all Israelis know by heart and smile when they hear it, says a lot about the Israeli improvisational culture. A common Hebrew expression is *"Yihyeh beseder"* (It'll be okay). This holds true even in situations in which we don't know what exactly awaits us. It is enough to rely on our faith, wisdom and optimism.

Between 2009 and 2012, I lived with my family in the city of Hoboken, New Jersey, in the United States. The winter of 2009 was particularly stormy. Coming from Israel, a hot country, I found the first winter very cold. By February I felt I had to get some sunshine as oxygen for my soul. I wanted to book a flight to Miami for the whole family for the following week. From there we would take a cruise to the Bahamas in the Caribbean. My husband told me I shouldn't be rash and emotional, but wait for a better opportunity. I insisted, and went ahead and bought the tickets.

The day before we were scheduled to leave, we heard on TV that all flights leaving the New York/New Jersey area were cancelled due to unusually stormy weather. I had no intention of calling off our trip! My goal was to revive myself in warm sunshine, and I would fight to achieve it. I contacted the airline and asked the customer service representative what my alternatives were. She just kept repeating that there were no other options. All the flights from the New York/New Jersey area had been cancelled.

Still on the phone, I tried to change my way of thinking about the situation, improvise and think outside the box. I asked her whether flights were leaving from Washington DC, a five-hour drive from where we lived. She said yes, they'd be taking off as usual. (At the time, I wondered why she hadn't thought of it herself.) So that's what we did. Not wanting to cancel our spontaneous vacation, we drove five hours to Washington, where we caught a flight to Miami.

The customer service representative was doing her job the way she had been taught, which evidently did not include striving to conceive of other possibilities. I, however, had been taught since childhood to be daring, not give up and always think creatively. And of course always to believe the Israeli mantra: "Yihyeh beseder" and **make it come true**.

Outside the Lines

The authors of the book "Border Crossings," Lucy Shahar and David Kurz, are Americans who immigrated to Israel. They put together a coloring book to describe the behaviors and attitudes of some Israelis:

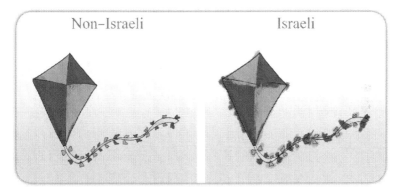

(Based on Shahar & Kurz, 2009, pp. 66-7)

Countries have rules and guidelines that citizens are expected to observe and follow for the sake of a smoothly running, orderly society. In many countries, such as the US, Britain, Germany, Switzerland and others, citizens remain "inside the lines," as depicted on the left-hand side of the above drawing. The downside is that sticking only to what is permitted leaves almost no room for improvisation.

In Israel, as shown on the right-hand side with coloring outside the lines, a high premium is placed on the ability to think outside the box. Israelis learn that it is perfectly acceptable and even preferable to improvise if it leads to a better outcome. In this regard, guidelines are perceived more as a suggestion than a necessity.

When one crosses the lines due to an improvisational mindset and thinking outside the box, the work plan, objectives and goals can all change, which may seem to create a mess. But at the same time, it can bring about better, more creative and interesting results.

In the Israeli business culture, the following attitudes and behaviors are favorably regarded:

- Willingness to push beyond limits.

- Willingness to improvise when it leads to achieving a better goal.

- Unlimited curiosity.

- Readiness to take a risk even if it stretches the boundary of the original plan.

> **Combina** *("combinot" in the plural) is an Israeli business phenomenon obviously referring to something along the lines of a combination. It usually involves recruiting different parties for a complicated project or deal, not necessarily but possibly with illegal elements. Combinot can also lead to skipping steps or failing to meet necessary standards. The phenomenon stems from the positive Israeli tendency to improvise and find creative solutions to overcome or circumvent problems or regulations.*

Case Study: Product Localization to Drive User Adoption

Moovit is an Israeli startup that offers real-time public transit information and GPS navigation including buses, ferries, trains and rapid transit (light rail, metro/subway/underground, etc.). The Moovit application is trusted by over 100 million users throughout more than 2,200 cities in 80 countries around the world.

When I visited Moovit's offices, I was impressed by the huge diversity among their employees: from Brazil, Germany, China and many other countries of origin. Employing people from different localities helps Moovit provide a high level of localization for their users. Yovav (Jay) Meydad (Moovit VP of Products & Marketing) shared with me how the company performs the vital work of localization.

Early on, Moovit used illustration graphics for their application icons, which saved them a lot of money and time. After switching to real pictures, their surveys showed a 50% rise in their active daily users. The most interesting change occurred when they replaced the pictures of generic buses with those of the actual local buses in each country; then their surveys showed a performance improvement of more than 100%! In other words, they listened to their target consumers' needs. Now, when local users see their own familiar buses or other means of transportation, they feel more comfortable and place more trust in the Moovit app, which is paramount in our global digital world.

In this case, Moovit's consumer market research and the consequent changes made to the app reflect the business potential embodied in the Israeli ability to improvise. The approach is to follow one logical step after another, and apply an open mind and the willingness to make modifications and upgrades. Just like with the entrepreneurial characteristic, we see here a kind of confidence and daring, without getting bogged down in overthinking and fear of the consequences.

Recommendation:

When working with Israelis, try to find the golden mean between your own careful planning and the Israeli ability to improvise and take risks. The different approaches can ultimately complement each other and lead to unforeseen, improved results.

There is a saying:

In America everything is allowed unless it is forbidden;

In Europe everything is forbidden unless it is allowed;

In Israel everything is allowed even if it is forbidden.

A Closer Look: Business as a Creative Pursuit

The two examples below show different aspects of the idea of improvisation. The first has to do with Israelis' tendency to invent their own ideas of specifications based on their own judgment. The second is more related to improvisation as a form of creativity, and its perception by Israelis as a positive value rather than an occasional unfortunate necessity or lack of preparedness.

On the Job: Airplane Maintenance Program

Ever since publishing the first edition of Israeli Business Culture in 2015, I have been receiving scores of emails from readers from all over the world who want to share their experiences working with Israelis. Here's an interesting one:

> Hi Osnat,
> I just finished reading your book "Israeli Business Culture" and enjoyed it very much.
> I'm currently involved in an aircraft conversion project in Israel. My company is converting one of our passenger airplanes to a cargo airplane and the Israeli company is contracted to do the conversion. As the on-site representative I interface with the Israeli management and personnel at Ben Gurion Airport. While all your anecdotes and recommendations in the book are true, my biggest challenge is having them, our contractor, comply with our company's FAA maintenance program

on the airplane. The Israelis don't seem to be concerned with our maintenance program policies and procedures since they are operating under their own conversion certification program. However, that's a risk to my company's FAA approved maintenance compliance. Other than my concern for compliance to our airline maintenance standards, I'm enjoying the experience immensely and find my Israeli counterparts easy to work with and consider them great friends.

Thanks again for the great insights in your book.

After receiving this email, I contacted the Israeli company, wanting to hear their side of the story, and to explain how our unconventional, improvisational way of thinking can sometimes be too creative in a highly regulated world and can paint us in an unprofessional light. In order to work better with other people, Israelis need to understand how they are perceived and maybe change some of their behavior. Unfortunately, I got no reply. That can also be common among Israelis...

When I contacted the author of the above letter to ask his permission to include it in this new edition of the book, he naturally agreed, and took the opportunity to further comment:

> "It is also worth adding that...we came through the challenges with mutual respect and I think as good friends. We're almost done and I'm certainly going to miss working with my friends and living in Israel. And one last thing, the Israeli company really knows how to throw a celebration commemorating an aircraft delivery!"

On the Job: Gourmet Soup Served in Disposable Tableware

Eyal Shani is an Israeli chef who owns the Romano, Hasalon, Port Said, North Abraxas and Miznon ("Diner") restaurants. He recently opened four more branches of the Miznon chain in New York, Paris, Vienna and Melbourne. Shani is known for his poetic language and straightforward, creative dishes. His unique expressiveness is evident in his appearances on various television programs as well as in the menus at his restaurants. Shani often presents his portions non-conventionally in Israel as well, for example: bread served on brown paper at his North Abraxas and Port Said eateries in Tel Aviv; and steak and even cauliflower tucked into pita bread at the Miznon restaurants.

Shani recently participated in the miniseries "Battle of the Chefs." He and fellow Israeli chef Yonatan Roshfeld flew together to Italy to study Italian production and cooking techniques, while the show focused on their close-up encounters. Each episode ended with a challenge that pitted the two of them head to head, with Italian master chefs judging the food they cook.

In the first episode of the series, Shani treated highly esteemed Neapolitan chefs to "country fish soup," served in blue plastic bowls that he had bought a few hours earlier at an outdoor market. Israelis love Eyal Shani's creative cuisine, but the Italian chefs were underwhelmed by his fish soup – because of its service in cheap plasticware.

Shani was subjected to harsh criticism not only for serving hot soup in plastic dishes but also of course for its inappropriateness at a traditional restaurant with white tablecloths. Of the Italian chefs' disapproval, Chef Shani said on camera, "Italians are incapable of understanding different presentation...Israelis understand me better because in Israel we demand progress, and evolving into something new..."

Model Synopsis and Recommendations

Once the honeymoon of initial professional contact is over, international businesspeople look for common social norms, core beliefs and sensitivity. In each culture, there will always be those who act somewhat differently. However, the majority of a country's population tends to behave in a similar manner, with the same behavior patterns and cultural assumptions. (See also, at the end of the Introduction: "Can We Avoid Cultural Generalizations?")

Following is a summary of the main Israeli business culture characteristics, using the word ISRAELI™ as an acronym for a practical guide in doing business with Israelis. This is an abbreviated version of Part 2 for quick reference, with brief, important tips:

I   Informal

S   Straightforward

R   Risk-Taking

A   Ambitious

E   Entrepreneurial

L   Loud

I   Improvisational

Informal

Informality in the Israeli business world is expressed not only in outward signs such as casual dress in the workplace, but also in the way people interact. In preliminary meetings or work interviews an Israeli might easily ask questions about your personal life, such as whether you are married or have children. In a low power distance culture like Israel, people also address one another by nicknames. Even Prime Minister Benjamin Netanyahu is called by his nickname, Bibi. Using such monikers gives both sides a feeling of closeness and maybe even friendship.

Advice for managers working with Israelis:
Cascade power down: Try to push power down through the organization and step out of the way. This will motivate your Israeli employees and also make them respect you for trusting and challenging them.

Advice for Israeli managers working with more formal cultures:
Use a more formal business approach: Allow your employees address you formally, using Ms. or Mr. plus your family name. Also, understand that your non-Israeli subordinates may expect and need your approval in order to move forward. If you don't adopt this approach, managers and employees from hierarchical cultures will see you as a weak and ineffective leader.

Straightforward

In Israeli culture you don't have to dig deep to understand where the other person stands. What they say is what they mean. When an Israeli thinks you are mistaken, he simply says, "You're wrong." When an Israeli invites you to his home, he expects you to arrive. When you ask for his opinion, he assumes you really want it, and gives you an honest and straightforward answer.

Advice for managers working with Israelis:
Differentiate between directness in business and personal sensitivity: Many Israelis are unaware of how aggressive their straightforwardness can appear to non-Israelis. Try to keep this in mind, and differentiate between directness in business and personal sensitivity.

Advice for Israeli managers working with less straightforward cultures:
Aim for harmony and use friendly words: Disagreement with the other can be expressed in a diplomatic sentence such as, "What you are suggesting sounds interesting. Let's discuss it in the future." People from less direct cultures learn such tactful, evasive remarks at an early age. Don't see them as dishonest. Respect their culture and their belief in the importance of harmony. Read between the lines and remember that friendly words with broad meanings like "interesting" or "in the future" are usually euphemisms for negative answers. A true intention for future collaboration will be expressed with a specific timeline.

Risk-Taking, Ambitious and Entrepreneurial

The next three characteristics are treated as one unit, since the combination of risk-taking and ambition jointly create the characteristic of entrepreneurialism, and form an integral part of it. An entrepreneur is an individual with the ambition to successfully create something new and the willingness to take risks to achieve it. Israel is a country of entrepreneurs seeking advancement. They are comfortable asking difficult questions and exploring all possibilities. They don't lose sight of their goals even if they don't always stick to rigid work plans or timetables.

Advice for managers working with Israelis:

Leverage potential benefits: Israelis tend to think big and aim high. Enjoy the possibility that their risk-taking and improvisation might pay off really well, but also remember that your ability for strategic long-term planning and attention to detail can serve as a balancing factor and valuable asset. That's also one example of why cultural diversity in an organization can increase real-time success.

Advice for Israeli managers working with cultures accustomed to more certainty:

Clarify and specify: Israelis work well in situations of uncertainty because they are, unfortunately, used to it in their daily lives, due to the political, security and economic situation in Israel. However, uncertainty and lack of order cause anxiety among many people from other cultures who are used to stability and clarity. To minimize this anxiety, Israelis should try and adopt the approach of first clarifying logical concepts in detail: why they believe in the project, how the risks have been calculated, what the next steps are, and so forth.

Loud

Loudness implies not only high volume, sharp intonations and forceful body language, but also the general feeling of intensity in Israel. The sense of "noise" everywhere comes from the multitudes of families walking down the streets, crowded roads and supermarkets. It also stems from the lack of personal space in Israel, reflected in constant touching and blunt questioning. In the business arena, there is no separation between personal and business life. Israelis may speak to family members and friends on the phone while at work and also put in long extra hours from home, including contacting colleagues during evening hours. All these in combination contribute to the impression that Israel and Israelis are "loud."

Advice for managers working with Israelis:

Try to accept the Israeli style and volume of communication without getting offended or overly distracted. Remember that in Israel people often get physically closer than you may feel comfortable with and tend to ask questions you may consider unprofessional. However, crossing borders in such ways is their cultural norm, and actually reflects interest and good will for building relationships.

Advice for Israeli managers working with cultures that find Israelis too "loud":

Respect personal space: Non-Israelis observe a clear border between private and public. Try to respect their personal space: physically not to come closer than 46 cm (18"), and emotionally not to ask private questions, like: How old are you? Do you have children? How much did that cost? How much do you make? and so forth.

Improvisational

The culture of improvisation in Israel supports "thinking outside the box." This means not just going along with an existing plan but continually thinking, initiating and changing until the desired goal is reached, especially in accordance with changes and challenges that arise along the way. Businesspeople in many countries are accustomed to working with a strict work plan and find it very challenging to accept Israelis' rapid changes.

Advice for managers working with Israelis:

Subdivide projects: When Israelis go outside the defined lines due to their improvisational mindset, the project outline, the timetable and even the goals can all change, which may seem to generate confusion. But their creative thinking can also bring about interesting and profitable results. I advise non-Israelis to clearly break down project stages so that any changes that come up can be monitored and discussed before moving on to the next step.

Advice for Israeli managers working with people accustomed to a strict plan:

Balance improvisation and planning: With coworkers and associates from cultures that advocate rigid work plans, try to find the golden mean between your own improvisational way of thinking and their careful planning. The different approaches can ultimately complement each other and lead to unforeseen, improved results. I also advise Israelis to subdivide each project into smaller parts to make sure that non-Israelis who are used to stricter work plans will be able to follow the changes and accept them.

Part 3

THE INTERPLAY OF ISRAELI™ CHARACTERISTICS

Part 3: The Interplay of ISRAELI™ Characteristics

Now that we've gone over the Israeli cultural characteristics in depth, let's focus more on how they play out in real time, beyond the many examples already given. Following are concrete insights, tips and tools that can assist managers, coworkers, vendors, clients and associates in improving communication and maximizing their work with Israelis, and probably with people from other cultures as well.

In this chapter we will answer questions such as:

Which tools can help us bridge the cultural gap?

What's the best way to manage culturally diverse teams?

What's the best way to lead virtual teams that include Israelis?

What are the 10 things that you need to know and expect when working with Israelis?

What are some cultural-specific insights for communication between Israelis and – respectively – Americans, Germans, Chinese and Africans?

We'll start with this true story about Israeli culture juxtaposed to American culture that I find both humorous and telling.

A young Israeli man working in an international company flies to the U.S. to meet an American colleague. They drive together to another company office, several hours away. On the way they stop to eat at a local fast food outlet. There is a long line inside. Out of the corner of his eye, the Israeli sees an employee sitting outside at the drive-thru window, waiting for vehicles. His Israeli personality immediately comes to the fore. He goes right over to the woman.

"Hello" he says, "the line inside is too long, and there are no cars outside at your window. Could I order from you?"

The employee, looking with amusement at the young man who has approached her on foot, says, "Sorry, sir, this station only serves customers in cars."

"Yes, I know," responds the Israeli, "but I thought that since the line inside is so long and there's no line out here, maybe you could help me out."

"Sir, our regulations say that I can only serve customers sitting in cars. Our insurance doesn't cover patrons outside their car at this window, so kindly go back inside and stand in line like everyone else."

The Israeli says thank you, takes two steps back and stops. He cannot give up. Why is the drive-thru window worker being so dogmatic? Why can't she bend the rules a little and help him? He decides to try again, this time using another strategy.

He goes back to her, with a big grin that he hopes will melt her resistance. Standing by the window, he gestures as if honking a car horn, calling out in a loud voice, "Toot...toot...toot..." as the worker stares at him in astonishment. Then the Israeli says, "Now, are you sure you won't take my order?"

The American employee most likely hasn't met many Israelis. What do you think she does? Does she take his order from the drive-thru window or not?

Well, unfortunately for him, she doesn't! But, being an Israeli, he derives some satisfaction from having tried. As I've mentioned, Israelis don't give up easily. But they also don't get too ruffled. You win some; you lose some.

Tools for Bridging the Cultural Gap

In my work, countless representatives of multinational companies have shared with me various challenges they've encountered when working with Israelis. However, sometimes the situation is extremely complex and I see these companies having trouble even just defining the gist of the difficulty they're facing, beyond the general. Following is an adapted process I have come up with that can help managers and employees from various cultures pinpoint and cope with cultural problems with Israelis.

Practical Problem Solving

An Ishikawa diagram, also known as a 'fishbone' diagram, is a map of causes and effects. It can help us identify the causes of a specific challenge.

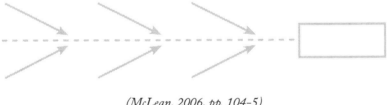

(McLean, 2006, pp. 104-5)

In the box at the right, you write the challenge that you or your organization is facing. In our case it is: Working with Israelis. Then you list all the possible causes you can think of, writing each cause next to one of the arrows. So we would list all the challenges we face while working with Israelis. For example:

- Israelis send short emails with not enough information.

- Israelis ask too many personal questions.

- Israelis tend to make rapid shifts from one subject to another during dialogue.

- Israelis put more emphasis on talking and less on listening.

- Israelis do not always follow the existing plan; they often change plans as the project progresses.

The next step is to choose the one most likely to be the root cause or primary arrow. This is now your new challenge to be addressed in another blank diagram, and also your first step in improving your multicultural working environment.

Now ask yourself four questions related to the challenge you are facing:

1. What do I expect from my Israeli colleagues?

2. What do the Israelis seem to expect from me?

3. What can I do to improve our working relations and business output?

4. What could they do to improve our working relations and business output?

188 | Israeli Business Culture

For example, let's take the challenge "correspondence with Israelis," where I send long, detailed emails, but the Israeli's replies are quite short, general and don't relate back to most of my questions.

1. What do I expect from my Israeli colleagues?

More details. Not just Yes or No answers with limited information.

Short answers give an impression of disinterest, lack of appreciation and/or unwillingness to cooperate. The quick, smooth advancement and ultimate success of the project partially depend on the Israelis expressing their commitment and communicating well.

2. What do the Israelis seem to expect from me?

Not to bother them with such long emails and too many details.

They expect me to just trust them and not put any pressure on them.

3. What can I do to improve our working relations and business output?

A good start would be to accept that English is not their mother tongue so it's harder for them to express themselves at length in writing in English. Most Israelis also prefer direct conversations over email correspondence. When I need to communicate or ask a question, I can call my Israeli colleagues on the phone (or go to their desks if we are in the same office). Besides immediately taking care of the business at hand, I might also try to explain how important it is for me to get more information and full answers to my questions.

4. What could Israelis do to improve our working relations and business output?

Ideally, Israelis will accept and follow through on the fact that businesspeople in other cultures are generally accustomed to receiving longer emails and more details (nice to know vs. need to know). Israelis need to make an effort to provide more details, and change their approach of "Don't worry, everything on my end is under control."

After filling out the diagram, answering the four questions posed above, and hopefully better understanding the problem, I recommend speaking with your Israeli colleague(s) in a physical or virtual face-to-face meeting, and pleasantly explaining your needs. Since most Israelis have...ahem, healthy egos, it's best to conduct this conversation informally and also provide positive reinforcement (compliments on their good points, expressions of professional appreciation for their work) while stressing the importance of good cooperation.

A few words of explanation and clarification can sometimes make all the difference in how one's attitude and behavior are perceived by others. Awareness of how you come across, as well as taking the time to explain what you are doing and why, can help build trust and significantly improve your business communication. The more you explain yourself, the more natural it becomes for your partner from the other culture to adjust to you. As with many challenges related to cross-cultural collaboration, understanding and open communication go a long way toward business success.

Cultural Smarts

As I've mentioned more than once, this book relates to research and generalizations about Israeli culture as well as other cultures. The generalizations apply to most people but it's important to remember that we are, above all, unique individuals. Therefore, when working with other cultures we have to behave not only with knowledge but also cultural intelligence. This enables harnessing the insights inherent in the rule while simultaneously treating each person as a special exception.

Good communication and cross-learning between cultures requires the involvement of bright individuals with high CQ (cultural intelligence). In "The Cultural Intelligence Difference" (2011), David Livermore writes that high cultural intelligence in global business is reflected in more than one's IQ, resume or technical expertise. The cultural intelligence model has four parameters.

CQ Parameters: Drive, Knowledge, Strategy and Action

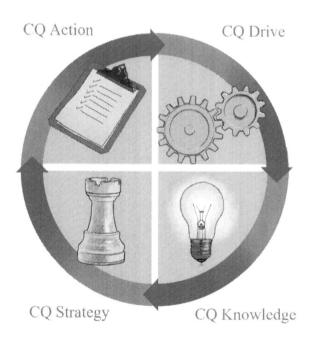

CQ Action   CQ Drive

CQ Strategy   CQ Knowledge

(Based on Livermore, 2011, pp. 41, 69, 107, 141)

CQ-Drive refers to one's interest and confidence in functioning effectively in culturally diverse settings.

CQ-Knowledge is the awareness of how other cultures resemble and differ from one's own.

CQ-Strategy refers to the way in which one makes sense of culturally diverse experiences. People need to assess their own thought processes as well as those of others.

CQ-Action is the ability to adapt verbal and nonverbal behavior to diverse cultures. It requires having a flexible repertoire of behavioral responses which suit a variety of cultural situations.

Cultural intelligence is no longer optional in today's global business arena. It is imperative for effective behavior in various situations that arise on a regular basis. Businesspeople who understand the importance of cross-cultural communication have the drive to learn about the behavior, norms and beliefs of any culture they do business with. Knowledge about the other person's culture as well as your own gives you the groundwork for strategic thinking. And when the time comes to take action, you are much better prepared regarding what to say, how to say it and to whom. I believe that your reading this book is a giant step forward in your acquiring the cultural knowhow and sensitivity to realize the full potential of a diverse workforce.

Managing Culturally Diverse Teams

Businesspeople need to have an understanding of cultural differences as well as know how to make the most of culturally diverse teams. Successful managers:

- Leverage positive cultural traits in individual team members.

- Use their own cultural intelligence to treat people from different cultures appropriately.

- Build trust relations with foreign employees and colleagues.

- Create an environment of involvement and respect.

- Build teamwork that reaps the benefits of different backgrounds, perspectives and ideas.

Working with empathy for one another enables mixed groups to generate greater business value.

Every worker, in any place or culture, is more productive in an atmosphere of acknowledgement and encouragement. Now that culturally mixed employees are common throughout the world, savvy managers need to understand the unique personal and cultural attributes among their workers in order to create a work environment that leads to business success.

For example, Americans, British and Germans employees expect clear directions from their management team. They may have trouble functioning and become stressed without explicit guidelines. However, Israelis employees look for empowerment. They require a reasonable amount of freedom and trust from their managers in order to thrive at their jobs.

Global businesspeople with a passion for diversity, a spirit for adventure and the self-confidence to tackle inclusion, take the extra step to learn about other cultures with an open mind and empathy; and they will be the leaders of tomorrow. They are the ones whose behavior, decisions and choices for building effective and profitable international organizations pave the way for succeeding in the contemporary global market.

---

2 Tips for Effective Management in Diverse Teams

When you are leading a diverse team, intercultural difficulty arises mainly in cases of criticism and when basic understanding of manager-employee expectations is lacking. Here are my recommendations:

1. **Listen impartially.**
   Let the other person explain their reasons for doing things a certain way. You'll learn a lot more that way than by automatically imposing your approach without respectfully hearing them out first.

2. **Be discreet.**
   Don't criticize an employee of any culture in front of his colleagues. Conduct any such conversation in private and remember to focus on the end results; no one is to blame.

   This seems to be the optimal way to forge an inclusive, mutually supportive team that benefits fantastically from all its individual members while meeting their needs and expectations.

A good manager explains what he expects from his employees. A good international manager adjusts his expectations to his employees' values and beliefs, based on the culture each individual comes from.

Leading Virtual Teams That Include Israelis

Leading any virtual team is quite challenging; and leading one that incorporates Israelis is much trickier. Virtual teams exist across physical and cultural boundaries. They share a common purpose, while mainly using web-based

(Photo: alphaspirit, n.d.)

means of communicating and collaborating, such as Slack (collaboration hub), Webex (online meetings and screen shares), GoToMeeting (HD video conferencing), Google Hangouts (instant messaging, video chat, SMS and VOIP features) and many other cool software programs for effective virtual team interaction. The obstacles to effective communication include the nonverbal components of messaging and email correspondence, different time zones and multiple languages. Moreover, remote trust-building is extremely challenging and quality control is obviously difficult.

For these among other reasons, strong leadership is essential for successful virtual teams. Managers need to:

- Build trust by providing an example of reliability and likeability

    - Reliability: when you say you will do something, do it

    - Likeability: get personal, including one-on-one feedback and sharing personal details about yourself

- Know what they want to achieve from any virtual meeting

    - Define the objective

    - Draft an agenda (stick to the timetable)

- Demand commitment and set deadlines for the team

    - Create clear tasks

    - Assign responsibility to prevent the bystander effect

All the above are much more challenging when the virtual team is composed of people from a variety of cultural backgrounds, specifically including Israelis, due to:

1. **The Israeli communication style**

    In the virtual group format with its absence of face-to-face interaction, respectfully listening to colleagues without interrupting is very important. Israelis' usual communication style, however, includes assertively cutting in, speaking loudly and using hand gestures to get the floor. When the emphasis is on politeness, many Israelis are at a disadvantage in getting their ideas across, and all the team members may feel misunderstood, offended and/or frustrated.

2. **Israeli informality**

    In virtual teams, it is vital to stick to pre-set meeting agendas and for the team to operate within strict time frames and work plans. There are no unplanned or informal social exchanges. Israelis, however, are masters of informal communication, so they find themselves at a loss when meetings are highly structured and formal. Many of their most valuable business interactions and brainstorming customarily take place next to the coffee machine or in the office hallway. In such physical settings they also have the option to engage in small talk, which is an integral part of the Israeli business culture. Furthermore, Israelis are at their most creative when they have the chance and flexibility to think outside the box and improvise.

Managing virtual teams draws on different skills than those required for co-located teams. Managers need high emotional and cultural intelligence to be able, in real-time, to adjust and solve the numerous tough situations that come up across spatial and cultural boundaries. The first key lies in understanding the prevailing cultural characteristics of the team members, as illustrated above.

10 Things to Expect
When Working with Israelis

Although many of the expectations vary due to a wide discrepancy in attitudes from one company to another, here are some expectations and small nuances that it may be helpful to be aware of when working with Israelis.

1. Building Motivation What motivates Israeli employees at work?	Responsibility, the challenge of overcoming obstacles, a sense of belonging, salary/bonuses, potential promotion.
2. Employees' Expectations What do Israeli employees expect from their management team?	Empowering them in the organization, trusting them, providing a reasonable amount of freedom, backing them up.
3. Managers' Expectations What do Israeli managers expect from their employees?	A "can do" attitude, commitment to deliver on assigned tasks, motivation, loyalty, openness, honesty, admitting and learning from mistakes, transparency.

4. Negotiation Style What is the customary negotiation style in Israel?	People-orientated, emotional expression, open confrontation (disagreement and debate), prioritizing the price, win-lose (one party benefits to the detriment of the other).
5. Topics for Conversation What topics do Israelis feel comfortable discussing with colleagues at work?	Israelis feel comfortable discussing almost anything. They will share information about their personal life (friends and family) at work. Salary, however, is usually taboo.
6. Performing Tasks What is the best way to ask an Israeli employee to perform a task? Do you generally need to double-check it?	Clearly explaining the task and the objective. Double-checking and status meetings are required.

7. Managerial Authority How is managerial authority received in Israel?	Respectfully (most of the time). Hierarchy exists, but it is okay to disagree with the manager openly, even in front of others. Still, the manager is the final decision-maker.
8. Work Evaluation Which parameters are evaluated in the Israeli work arena?	End results (success), caring and involvement, relationships, thinking outside the box, putting in extra time and effort.
9. Constructive Feedback What kind of feedback is most constructive for Israeli employees?	Feedback should be transparent and direct. Absolute descriptors are often used. Feedback is usually given in private but sometimes in front of a group.
10. Work-Life Balance What is the customary work-life balance in Israel?	Differs greatly in each company. People in the high-tech sector often work nights and weekends to adapt to global work days and time zones.

A Closer Look: Culture-Specific Insights

Bridging the Israeli-American Gap

The first step in enhancing communication and overcoming the Israeli-American cultural gap lies in understanding the main cultural characteristics of Americans and Israelis, and comparing the two. Then you'll start seeing how collaboration between the two cultures can became a whole that is bigger than the sum of its parts.

In Part 2 we discussed each characteristic of the Israeli business culture at great length. Now I will relate briefly to those characteristics again in comparison to American culture:

I is for Informal – not just how Israelis dress, but also how they communicate with one another.
Israelis feel very comfortable with their managers. A junior employee can engage in dialogue and even in an argument with his boss, even with other colleagues present. In the U.S., the hierarchy is much clearer and stricter. Respect is paid to superiors and if criticism is aired at all, it's only behind closed doors in a one-on-one meeting.

S is for Straightforward, because Israelis use a direct style of speech.
When an Israeli thinks you are mistaken, he simply says, "You're wrong." In the United States, disagreement tends to be expressed in more diplomatic sentences, such as, "What you are suggesting sounds interesting; what do you think about..." Israelis, who use

a much more direct style of speech, find it difficult to understand whether such friendly words express a genuine intent or not. They are accustomed to straight talking, which in the eyes of Americans can appear rude and aggressive. When working with Israelis, try to keep this in mind, and differentiate between directness in business and interpersonal sensitivity.

R is for Risk-Taking, A is for Ambitious, and E is for Entrepreneurial.

These three are interrelated, because an entrepreneur is someone with a great idea who also has the necessary ambition and drive to see it through, and who will take risks and do whatever it takes to reach their goal. Therefore, Israelis feel comfortable asking difficult questions and exploring all possibilities. They don't lose sight of their goals, even if they don't always stick to rigid work plans or timetables like most American businesspeople.

L stands for Loud.

Loud refers to not just the high volume but also the somewhat aggressive manner and intense atmosphere in Israel. Non-Israelis who visit Israel sense a lack of personal space, reflected in constant touching and frank questioning. Americans should understand that conducting business loudly doesn't necessarily mean there's an argument taking place or that the deal is in danger; it's just the Israeli manner and it shows enthusiasm for the topic of the conversation. For Americans, raising one's voice in the workplace is considered unprofessional or at least overly dramatic and uncomfortable for others. Politeness is standard business behavior in the U.S. but still a developing concept in Middle Eastern Israel.

The last I is for Improvisational, because Israelis are creative, adaptable and always try to think outside the box.
In the U.S., people proceed according to work plans and find it very challenging to accept Israelis' rapid changes in plans. In culturally diverse groups, it's worthwhile to subdivide each project into smaller parts, to make sure that Americans can follow the changes before moving on to the next step. At the same time, consider that Israeli-style improvisation, although sometimes challenging, can also lead to many great ideas, fast progress and outstanding results.

With this clearer view of the gaps between the American and Israeli cultures, it should be easier to have more empathy and respect when communicating, and to take advantage of each culture's strong points for even better business success.

Bridging the Israeli-German Cultural Gap

German businesspeople have lately been showing increasing interest in Israel. In the past few years I've flown to Germany a number of times to lead workshops for some very appealing German companies. I've also been interviewed by professional journals based in Germany. More business between two countries always means a greater need of good cross-cultural communication skills!

In 2016, 11 MBA students from the Munich Marketing Academy visited Israel to experience the latter country's dynamic business environment. Their group consisted of experienced professionals in IT, marketing, sales, technology, entertainment and the health care industry. They met with Israeli companies and organizations such as Weissbeerger, Fortvision, Gauzy, SoftWheels, the Israel-German Chamber of Commerce and myself, at OLM Consulting. At our meeting, we spoke at great length about the German-Israeli cultural gap as well as their first impressions of Israel.

Here is a sampling of their reflections on their time in Israel:

Chris (head of marketing) was very excited to see the "no-fear mentality" in Israel. This Israeli characteristic is also reflected in the attitude that it's okay to admit failure and that you also gain experience from past failures in order to improve in the future.

Pascal (field representative) added that it was wonderful to see so many Germans products in Israel and that, more than 70 years after World War II and the Holocaust, Israeli people can move

206 | Israeli Business Culture

forward, without forgetting, and work with Germans in such a delightful way. He also mentioned how the people in Israel are very open, with a friendly look in their eyes.

Oliver (VP of corporate communication) said he felt that Israel is the place where Silicon Valley meets the European business style, with less formality. He also emphasized that Israeli entrepreneurs bear the international market in mind from the very beginning. Since the domestic market in Israel is so small, Israelis always think in terms of the global market, which saves on later adaptations.

Rike (sales and marketing manager) said that visiting Israel is great for a bit of business inspiration and gaining new ideas, impressions and possibilities. She remarked that Israelis are kindly welcoming, open-minded and always busy.

Daniel (consultant) spoke about Israeli chutzpah, which he finds to be a mixture of purposeful, intelligent effrontery, charming sharpness and irresistible audacity. And he liked it. He feels that in Israel we don't waste time by "talking around the subject"; the sense and purpose of any conversation is clarified early on, without any detours.

Although German people are considered to use a direct style of speech, like Israelis, there are differences between the two styles. Israelis are much more emotional when they talk, so they sound more direct and assertive. Furthermore, Germans organize their thoughts before expressing them out loud, whereas Israelis don't usually take that extra step.

Many Israelis seldom prepare for discussions or any-sized projects in the business arena. They improvise a lot and run straight from getting a good idea into its execution, with little time for planning. Germans typically view the planning process as a very important part of any project, and therefore invest much time and money in that stage.

This situation is challenging when it comes to communication between the two cultures. But with mutual awareness of all these differences and proper collaboration, both sides in joint projects can benefit from and enjoy the advantages of both valuable approaches. They can choose when it is right to plan in greater detail and when it is appropriate to plunge into improvisation and take risks.

Bridging the Israeli-Chinese Cultural Gap

Israel and China have a relationship, and just like in every love story, what excited you at first is exactly what bothers you the most, further down the line.* Israeli-Chinese relations are somewhat complex. On one hand, the Chinese come to Israel in masses to study entrepreneurism and thinking outside the box. On the other hand, the Chinese culture is vastly different from the Israeli culture and does not facilitate rapid change.

The typical Israeli rush to immediately manufacture every idea is the polar opposite of conservative Chinese culture. The Chinese advocate precision, respect and hierarchy, and their culture calls for forging a personal connection and trust before doing business

---

* Material originally published in Asia Times (Lautman, 2016).

together, which, of course, takes time. In the world of Israeli innovation there is no time to lose, nor any hierarchy, nor any polite distance. Attention to detail often comes through trial and error, with a lot of other risk-taking along the way.

Asia Times has published many articles regarding business interests between China and Israel: "China And Israel's Tale Of Love And High-Tech"; "Building Relations: Israel plans to hire 20,000 Chinese construction workers"; "How Shimon Peres Built the China-Israel Relationship" and others. However, do Israelis have any idea how their business behavior is perceived by the Chinese? And, conversely, are the Chinese aware of the main Israeli traits in business and the most effective way of working with Israelis?

The two countries have synergistic relations. Chinese customers are interested in Israel, and Israeli customers would like to work in China. Although China is huge and Israel is tiny, Israel has vast knowledge in research and development, particularly in medicine, water purification, agriculture and other key realms. Many Chinese are keen to learn from this know-how and cooperate with Israelis, while the Israelis obviously understand the massive potential of the market in China. (It wasn't just by chance or on a whim that I had the first edition of my book translated into Mandarin Chinese as the only other language besides English, so far.)

It's important to remember that Israeli impatience and spontaneity are part of the same innovative culture that generated the country's hyper-developed high-tech industry, and part of the same rough, informal culture that put many Chinese people off Israelis. Chinese want to slowly build up trust relations with their colleagues and customers, and Israelis are in a constant hurry to conquer the world. In Israel every employee feels and acts like a know-it-all manager, loudly and bluntly offering their professional opinion to one and all.

It's acceptable in Israel to say you don't understand something and considered okay when a manager stretches and tests your limits to the very end. It's also fine to fail, since you learn from every failure and subsequently improve. In China, if you push your employee beyond his capabilities and he fails, you may have insulted his honor and caused him to lose motivation to do the project. Perhaps he will also lose faith in you as a manager.

Israel and China are most definitely in a relationship. Being in love and getting the most out of each other is hard work. The Chinese and the Israelis need to learn more about each other's business cultures. Understanding leads to empathy (and flexibility, even forgiveness), which in turn brings about mutual business success, which translates into almost "boundless" love.

Bridging the African-Israeli Cultural Gap

I recently had the privilege of conducting a cross-cultural communication workshop for a global Israeli company. The workshop participants were employees from West Africa and Central Africa, together with their colleagues in Israel. I decided the best approach would be to start by giving the Africans the stage to share their local culture as well as their challenges in working with Israelis.

Culture can be defined in many different ways: the characteristics and mindset of a certain group, everything from language, religion, food, habits, arts and more to values, beliefs and social norms. It is a combination of what we see above the surface, including our verbal and non-verbal communication, and—even more important—what exists below the surface, such as our underlying assumptions and worldview.

In the workshop, I divided the participants into three groups based on their countries of origin: West Africans, Central Africans and Israelis. I asked each group to list the ten main values and cultural characteristics in their own country. Here are their lists:

ISRAEL

Creativity
Resilience
Directness
Dynamism
Improvisation
Competitiveness
Aggressiveness
Ambition
Informality
Warmth

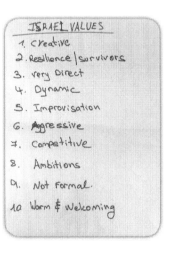

WEST AFRICA

(participants from Niger, Burkina Faso and Senegal)

Hospitality
Hard working
Honesty
Religion
Tradition
Flexibility
Family solidarity
Quietness
Communicativeness
Patriotism

CENTRAL AFRICA

(participants from Cameroon, Ivory Coast
and the Republic of the Congo)

Hospitality
Integration
Peacefulness
Dynamism
Laicity [religious tolerance]
Informality
Flexibility with time
Tradition
Respect for the old
Multiculturalism

The discussion about the similarities and the differences in each group was illuminating; however, most notable was the conversation between the West African and Central African participants. Due to their high diversity (for example, some countries have more than 200 dialects), they felt free to speak openly and honestly about the difficulties in Africa and the differences among the various groups. This multiplicity is both one of Africa's greatest beauties and one of its biggest obstacles to becoming a stronger continent, socioeconomically speaking.

We learned in the workshop that each country in Africa is represented by an animal. Cameron, for example, is a lion, Burkina Faso a horse, the Ivory Coast an elephant, and so forth. We Israelis thought to ourselves: Which animal would best represent Israel? One of the participants said "cat" and I liked that idea, since we always land on our feet. But we decided we also had to consider the small size of our country, so maybe it would be better to go with an ant because we are so diligent, or perhaps a bee because we make so much noise and never-ending buzz...

Israelis need to be heard. We are constantly confronting one another, and with a lot of emotion. West Africans and Central Africans can also get quite emotional when speaking to each other, but some of them are more comfortable with that trait than others. I had the participants add their nations' flags on a printed map of Erin Meyer's four-quadrant matrix. Note how the African countries are not just culturally divergent from Israel but from one another as well.

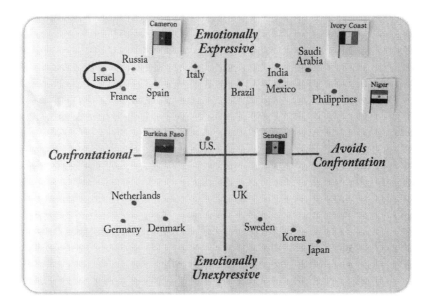

Most important is to work with empathy and understand that people from different countries have different values. We need to communicate with high cultural intelligence in order to build a diverse team in which the whole is greater than the sum of its parts. This means keeping an open mind, maximizing each culture's strong points and not taking offense at behavior you wouldn't normally—meaning in your own culture—consider "acceptable," "polite" or "necessary."

A Personal Story, Conclusions and New Beginnings

A Chance Meeting at a Tel Aviv Restaurant

Noam Lanir is one of the most successful entrepreneurs in Israel (see "The Founding Generation" in Part 2). In tiny Israel, I happened to run into him when my husband and I went to the Dinings, a prestigious Japanese restaurant located on the roof of the Norman Hotel in Tel Aviv. After glancing at the menu, we quickly grasped that the prices were way beyond our everyday budget. Nevertheless, we stayed to enjoy a glass of wine and the atmosphere. Ofra Strauss, chairwoman of Strauss, the second largest Israeli food manufacturer, was seated a few tables away from us; and sitting right near me, at the bar, was...Noam Lanir.

Now I admit that I was not personally acquainted with Lanir, and it took a bit of Israeli chutzpah for me to go up to him, touch his shoulder, and say, "Noam Lanir, it's a pleasure to meet you. My name is Osnat Lautman!" Before I had even finished speaking, he stood up, smiled broadly, and said, "And what is your connection to the charming Dov Lautman?"

Dov Lautman, who passed away in November of 2013, was an industrialist and Israeli businessman. He founded and owned the Delta Galil textile plants, and was a president of the Israel

Manufacturers' Association and an Israel Prize laureate for Lifetime Achievement – Special Contribution to Society and the Nation. I'm sure that such a family connection could have helped me access many businesspeople, such as Noam Lanir. But, the truth is, I am not related to Dov Lautman. My grandfather did go visit him years ago in an attempt to locate family members after the Holocaust, but after a few hours of nice hospitality they finally realized there was no familial connection between these two branches of Lautmans.

When Noam Lanir stood up at the sound of my name, I smiled as well. That's just the way it is in Israel. Quite a few people at the top of the Israeli business, political and military worlds know each other. I told Lanir in amusement that he could sit down; I had no connection to Dov Lautman and had approached him because of a book I had written in which he is mentioned.

I told Lanir that the book, Israeli Business Culture, includes a practical model that uses the letters in the word "Israeli" as a basis for organizing the characteristics of Israeli business culture. I also explained that his success story in the section on entrepreneurialism describes how Lanir, as a successful entrepreneurial business figure, possesses farseeing vision, the ability to turn his dreams into reality against all odds and a talent for making difficult, intuitive decisions. The fact that he started as a public relations advisor for Tel Aviv nightclubs and over the years, up through today, has been the founder and/or a senior officer in various exceptional companies, makes his life story and business success even more amazing.

After Lanir heard all I had to say and saw the digital file of my book on my mobile device, he rose once again and gave me a giant hug, whispering in my ear, "This is an Israeli businesswoman. This is Israeli culture....This is Israeli chutzpah!!" He took my phone number and promised to read more from the book and then send me his comments. Although I haven't heard from him, at least not yet, I think that this encounter provided me with another great anecdote.

Many of the salient points in my model were expressed in that spontaneous meeting that only a lasted a few minutes: our informal dialogue (not to mention casual attire, including flip-flops and a non-button-down shirt in a fancy restaurant); the straightforwardness of the way I approached Lanir and what we both said; loudness, not in volume but in the crossing boundaries of personal space – my touch on his shoulder and the warm parting embrace; and of course the improvisational moment – my seizing the opportunity for an interesting conversation, one which provides a lot of food for thought.

Prevalent traits and behaviorisms in Israeli culture are often perceived as aggressive and unpleasant, and the Yiddish-Hebrew term "chutzpah" (audacity) has become an internationally-known word. This book has covered the Israeli values and norms that lead to a certain kind of conduct. Using the knowledge you have gained, you are likely to be more understanding and less judgmental when working with Israelis. You can discern not only the chutzpah but also the determination, ambitiousness and original, bold thinking that is so common among Israelis.

Cultural Mindfulness

> "Mindfulness is paying attention in a particular way, on purpose, in the present moment, non-judgmentally."
>
> – *Prof. Jon Kabat-Zinn (qtd by Mindful Staff, 2017)*

Mindfulness is vital in a multicultural environment. In the professional arena, it is a way of being fully present with yourself and in your diverse relationships at work. It creates clarity, self-observation and an even better understanding of how other cultures view our culture. Building upon this concept, it's important to understand your own identity and culture, and then outspread this knowledge into deeper awareness of other cultures and ethnicities.

Mindfulness includes awareness with the willingness to listen to others and learn from them, without judgment of right or wrong!

I recommend bringing more mindfulness to our personal and professional lives. Not labeling or criticizing the different cultures around us, but embracing, accepting, joining together and learning from them. We can be more sensitive to our surroundings if we put our minds to it.

A Final Word of Advice...

The number of international companies in Israel, and of Israeli companies working with people all over the world, is helping Israelis learn about other cultures. Indeed, in recent years Israelis are demonstrating higher awareness of cultural differences, along with a desire to adjust their behavior with empathy and mindfulness for the sake of reducing cultural gaps to further their success in business.

I suggest aiming for good communication with Israelis, and not getting insulted by dialogue that may be informal, overly direct, or otherwise characteristic of Israeli interactions. Instead of taking their behavior personally, you can view it as an opportunity for open communication. Be culture clever. This approach will smooth the way for successful business dealings that transcend geographical and cultural boundaries.

Good luck!

Thank you for reading the book.

As you may have realized, this second edition actually came about due to the great and plentiful feedback I received from readers who wished to share with me their personal experiences with Israelis in the workplace and business arena. I'm naturally very grateful to all those contributors, and invite you to also enlighten me – and eventually other readers as well, through my blogs and books – with your own relevant stories.

Please feel free to visit my website, olm-consulting.com, and to contact me at:

Email: osnat@olm-consulting.com

LinkedIn profile: Osnat Lautman Mansoor

Facebook page: Israeli Business Culture; OLM-Consulting

References

Alba, A. (2016, April 11). A conversation with Uri Levine: Advice, anecdotes from the man who sold Waze to Google for $1.1 billion. *NY Daily News*. Retrieved from www.nydailynews.com/news/national/advice-uri-levine-man-sold-waze-1-1b-article-1.2596074

Alefbet. (n.d.). Fabric succah decorated... [Royalty-free stock image]. *Shutterstock*. Retrieved from https://www.shutterstock.com/image-photo/fabric-sukkah-decorated-printed-pattern-hebrew-540430642

Alphaspirit. (n.d.). Social network connection... [Royalty-free stock image]. *Shutterstock*. Retrieved from https://www.shutterstock.com/image-photo/social-network-connection-between-men-women-247679242

Avriel, Eytan. (2015, June 11). These are the 500 richest people in Israel. Haaretz. Retrieved from https://www.haaretz.com/israel-news/business/.premium-who-are-the-500-richest-israelis-1.5371205

Barak, O., & Sheffer, G. (2013). *Israel's security networks: A theoretical and comparative perspective*. Cambridge, UK: Cambridge University Press.

Berman, A. (2013, February 28). ISRAEL: The godfather of Israeli high tech. *San Diego Jewish Journal*. Retrieved from http://sdjewishjournal.com/sdjj/march-2013/israel-the-godfather-of-israeli-high-tech/

CBS. (2017, December 31). Press release: Population of Israel on the eve of 2018 - 8.8 million. [In Hebrew]. *Central Bureau of Statistics*. Retrieved from http://www.cbs.gov.il/reader/newhodaot/hodaa_template.html?hodaa=201711387.

Cohen, D. (n.d.). Hasidic ultra-Orthodox Jewish children... [Royalty-free stock image]. *Shutterstock*. Retrieved from https://www.shutterstock.com/image-photo/hasidic-ultra-orthodox-jewish-children-look-1017833515

Doing Business. (2016, October 25). Doing business 2017: Equal opportunity for all. *The World Bank*. Retrieved from http://www.doingbusiness.org/reports/global-reports/doing-business-2017.

Finkler, K. (2018, March 19). Independence trail in Tel Aviv. [In Hebrew]. *Channel 7*. Retrieved from www.inn.co.il/News/News.aspx/368898

Gideon, K./GPO Israel. (2017, July 4). Ruby Rivlin presented certificates... [Cropped digital image]. Wikimedia Commons [License: https://creativecommons.org/licenses/by-sa/3.0/legalcode]. Retrieved from https://commons.wikimedia.org/wiki/File:Ruby_Rivlin_presented_certificates_of_excellence_to_the_outstanding_officers_of_the_Shin_Bet_(GPO704).jpg

Haaretz. (2016, September 28). Shimon Peres on life, war, and Israel: 10 best quotes [Quoted from Peres' biography of David Ben-Gurion]. *Haaretz*. Retrieved from https://www.haaretz.com/israel-news/shimon-peres-on-life-war-and-israel-10-best-quotes-1.5443972

Hacohen, Y. (2010, November 30). Surprising? 93 percent light Hanukkah candles. [In Hebrew]. *B'Chadrei Chadarim*. Retrieved from http://www.bhol.co.il/news/77048

Hall, E. T. (1959). *The silent language*. New York, NY: Doubleday.

---. (1966). *The hidden dimension*. New York, NY: Doubleday.

---. (1967). *Beyond culture*. New York, NY: Anchor Press.

Halperin, I. (2013, December 20). Israel: at the forefront of global innovation. Grant Thornton. Retrieved from http://www.grantthornton.com.mx/en/insights/blogs/blog-at-the-forefront-of-global-innovation/

Hartog, K. (2018, June 11). Stars come out in Hollywood to celebrate Israel's 70th anniversary. *The Jerusalem Post*. Retrieved from www.jpost.com/Diaspora/Stars-come-out-in-Hollywood-to-celebrate-Israels-70th-anniversary-559675

Hofstede, G. (1991). *Cultures and organizations: Software of the mind*. New York, NY: McGraw-Hill.

IDF/Matanya. (2011, March 28). Iron dome battery deployed near Ashkelon [Israel Defense Forces photograph uploaded on September 19, 2011]. *Wikipedia Commons*

[License: https://creativecommons.org/licenses/by/2.0/ legalcode]. Retrieved from https://he.wikipedia.org/wiki/ קובץ:Iron_Dome_Battery_Deployed_Near_Ashkelon. jpg

JekLi (n.d.). The Temple Mount... [Royalty-free stock image]. *Shutterstock*. Retrieved from https://www.shutterstock. com/image-photo/temple-mount-western-wall-golden-dome-519093583?src=URE3lbiU1U0qDli-mNaj7g-1-2

Jerusalem Institute. (2017). Population. Jerusalem: Facts and trends 2017 – The state of the city and changing trends. Retrieved from en.jerusaleminstitute.org.il/.upload/ publications/Jeruslaem%20Facts%20and%20Trends%20 -%202.Population.pdf

Kalman, M. (2013, August 12). Israeli military intelligence unit drives country's hi-tech boom. *The Guardian*. Retrieved from www.theguardian.com/world/2013/aug/12/israel-military-intelligence-unit-tech-boom

Knesset website. (n.d.). Proclamation of Independence. Available from www.knesset.gov.il/docs/eng/megilat_eng.htm

Kolodetsky, Menachem. (2017). CBS data: Only 9% ultra-Orthodox in Israel. [In Hebrew]. *Actualic News*. Retrieved from http://actualic.co.il/9--רק-הלמס-נתוני אחוז-חרדים-במדינה/

Lautman, O. (2016, December 20). China & Israel business relations: A love upgrade. *Asia Times*. *Retrieved from* www. atimes.com/china-israel-business-relations-love-upgrade/

Layes, G. (2010). Intercultural learning and acculturation. In *Handbook of intercultural communication and cooperation* (2nd ed.). A. Thomas, E. Kinast, & S. Schroll-Machl (Eds). Göttingen, Germany: Vandenhoeck & Ruprecht.

LeWeb. (2011, December 9). Yossi Vardi... [Digital image]. *Flickr* [License: https://creativecommons.org/licenses/by/2.0/legalcode]. Retrieved from https://www.flickr.com/photos/leweb3/6482015301

Lewis, R. D. (1996). *When cultures collide: Managing successfully across cultures.* London, UK: Nicholas Brealey Publ.

Lightspring. (n.d.). Drawing a bridge... [Royalty-free stock image]. *Shutterstock.* Retrieved from https://www.shutterstock.com/image-illustration/drawing-bridge-conquering-adversity-business-concept-347537057

Liorpt. (n.d.). Tel Aviv skyline... [Stock image ID: 610983042]. iStock [Standard license]. Retrieved from https://www.istockphoto.com/il/photo/tel-aviv-skyline-aerial-photo-gm610983042-105046601

Livermore, D. (2011). *The cultural intelligence difference. American Management Association.* New York, NY: AMACOM.

McClean, Z. J. (n.d.). Israeli sabih [Royalty-free stock image]. *Shutterstock.* Retrieved from https://www.shutterstock.com/image-photo/israeli-sabih-666256042?src=y5G9beefBn7Z8hh1ciWu3w-1-2

McLean, G. N. (2006). *Organization development: Principles, processes, performance.* Oakland, CA: Berrett-Koehler.

Meyer, E. (2014). *The culture map: Breaking through the invisible boundaries of global business.* New York, NY: PublicAffairs.

-----. (2015, December). Getting to si, ja, oui, hai, and da. *Harvard Business Review.* Retrieved from hbr.org/2015/12/getting-to-si-ja-oui-hai-and-da

Mishella. (n.d.). Declaration of Independence... [Royalty-free stock image]. *Shutterstock.* Retrieved from https://www.shutterstock.com/image-photo/declaration-independence-state-israel-1948-34558216?src=i2Fvm WC63aE37mrr5ZHpMw-1-4

Mindful Staff. (2017, January 11). Jon Kabat-Zinn: Defining mindfulness. *Mindful.* Retrieved from www.mindful.org/jon-kabat-zinn-defining-mindfulness/

Nachshoni, K. (2016, October 9). Yom Kippur 5777: 61% will fast, 38% will pray. [In Hebrew]. *Ynet.* Retrieved from https://www.ynet.co.il/articles/0,7340,L-4864015,00.html

Peretz, S. (2010, August 4). The Israeli genome: What makes Israeli entrepreneurs so successful?" [In Hebrew]. *Globes.* Retrieved from www.globes.co.il/news/article.aspx?did=1000579269.

Pridan, M. (1958, April 25). IL declaration re-enactment 1958 [Public domain digital image]. *Wikimedia Commons.*

Retrieved from https://commons.wikimedia.org/wiki/
File:IL_Declaration_re-enactment1958.jpg

Quora. (2012, July 3). Why are Israeli people so hard to work
with? Retrieved from www.quora.com/Why-are-Israeli-
people-so-hard-to-work-with/

Rabi, I. (2015, September 20). Israel best investment after Silicon
Valley – Deloitte." *Globes*. Retrieved from www.globes.
co.il/en/article-deloitte-israel-best-for-investment-
after-silicon-valley-1001069595

Rathje, S. (2015, May 20). Multicollectivity. [Slideshow]. *SIETAR
Europa Congress 2015*. Retrieved from https://www.
sietareu.org/images/stories/congress2015/presentations/
Saturday/Rathje_Multicollectivity.pdf

Rawpixel.com. (n.d.). Alarm timing clock... [Digital image].
Shutterstock. Retrieved from https://www.shutterstock.
com/image-photo/alarm-timing-clock-schedule-
punctual-time-523875211

Rottier, B., Ripmeester, N., and Bush, A. (2011). Pediatric
Pulmonology, 46, 409–411. Retrieved from http://
www.labourmobility.com/wp-content/uploads/2011/07/
Pedriatic_Pulmonoly_finalversion.pdf

Schiff, R. L. (1992). Civil-military relations reconsidered: Israel
as an 'uncivil' state. *Security Studies, 1*(4), 636-658.

Schmidl, E. (2012, May 11). Zuckerberg slammed for wearing
hoodie on IPOroadshow. *Smart Company*. Retrieved from

www.smartcompany.com.au/people-human-resources/
leadership/zuckerberg-slammed-for-wearing-hoodie-
on-ipo-roadshow-but-what-do-local-entrepreneurs-
think-about-dress-codes/

Schwartz, N. (2015, May 11). Cavaliers coach David Blatt
compares himself to a fighter pilot. *USA Today*. Retrieved
from ftw.usatoday.com/2015/05/david-blatt-fighter-
pilot-lebron-james-cavaliers

Senor, D., & Singer, S. (2009). *Start-up nation: The story of Israel's
economic miracle*. New York, NY: Twelve Books.

Shahar, L., & Kurz, D. (1995). *Border crossings*. London, UK:
Nicholas Brealey Publ.

Sherki, Y. (2015, November 11). The videotaped will that
Navon left behind. [In Hebrew]. *Mako*. Retrieved from
https://www.mako.co.il/news-channel2/Channel-2-
Newscast-q4_2015/Article-66efecad228f051004.htm

SigDesign. (n.d.). Israel memorial day and independence
day... [Royalty-free stock image]. *Shutterstock*.
Retrieved from https://www.shutterstock.com/image-
vector/israel-memorial-day-independence-banner-
sadness-1036140271

Teicher, A. (2009, May 28). Statue of Mayor Meir Dizengoff...
[Digital image]. *Wikipedia*. Retrieved from https://
he.m.wikipedia.org/wiki/קוב:Statue_of_Mayor_Meir_
Dizengoff_on_a_Horse_in_Tel_-Aviv.jpg

-----. (2015, September 25). Sculpture of David Ben Gurion... [Digital image]. *Wikimedia Commons* [License: https://creativecommons.org/licenses/by/2.5/legalcode]. Retrieved from https://commons.wikimedia.org/wiki/File:PikiWiki_Israel_45054_Sculpture_of_David_Ben_Gurion_in_Tel_Aviv_beach.JPG

The World in HDR. (n.d.). Colorful picture of Knesset... [Royalty-free stock image]. *Shutterstock*. Retrieved from https://www.shutterstock.com/image-photo/colorful-picture-knesset-israel-israeli-parliament-336166106

Todorovic, A. (n.d.). Panoramic view Tel Aviv... [Royalty-free stock image]. *Shutterstock*. Retrieved from https://www.shutterstock.com/image-photo/panoramic-view-telaviv-public-beach-on-101887351?src=SVp0_EWuA71bK0Sifxcz1A-1-4

Tsalani, D. (2014, June 18). Your ultimate guide to minimum viable product (+great examples). *Fast Monkeys – Official Blog*. Retrieved from blog.fastmonkeys.com/2014/06/18/minimum-viable-product-your-ultimate-guide-to-mvp-great-examples/

US State Department. (2018, April. 29). Benjamin Netanyahu April 2018 [Public domain cropped digital image]. *Wikimedia Commons*. Retrieved from https://commons.wikimedia.org/wiki/File:Benjamin_Netanyahu_April_2018.jpg

Wierzba. (2010, March 16). Yitzhak Navon [Public domain cropped digital image]. *Wikipedia*. Retrieved from https://he.wikipedia.org/wiki/קובץ:Yitzhak_Navon_1.jpg

World Economic Forum. (2005). Shimon Peres 2005 [Cropped digital image]. *Wikimedia Commons* [License: https://creativecommons.org/licenses/by-sa/2.0/legalcode]. Retrieved from https://commons.wikimedia.org/wiki/File:Shimon_Peres_2005.jpg

World Population Review. (2018). Tel Aviv population 2018. Retrieved from http://worldpopulationreview.com/world-cities/tel-aviv-population/

Yanay, K. (2016, January 27). 19 fascinating Hebrew words that don't have any direct translation in English. *Thought Catalog*. Retrieved from thoughtcatalog.com/kiley-yanay/2016/01/19-beautiful-hebrew-words-that-dont-have-any-direct-translation-in-english/)

Yaakov, Saar/GPO. (1994, November 24). The Nobel Peace Prize laureates… [Digital image]. Flickr [License: https://creativecommons.org/licenses/by-sa/3.0/legalcode]. Retrieved from https://he.m.wikipedia.org/wiki/קובץ:Flickr_-_Government_Press_Office_(GPO)_-_THE_NOBEL_PEACE_PRIZE_LAUREATES_FOR_1994_IN_OSLO..jpg

Yehoshua, Y. (2014, August 7). Lieutenant Eitan ran to the tunnel: 'I don't want a medal, I'm no hero. This is what's expected of every combat soldier. [In Hebrew]. *YNet*. Retrieved from www.ynet.co.il/articles/0,7340,L-4555865,00.html

Ynet. (2014, April 4). 94% conduct a Seder; 56% say the leavened products law is essential. [In Hebrew]. *Ynet*. Retrieved from https://www.ynet.co.il/articles/0,7340,L-4212338,00. html

Zeltzer-Zubida, A., & Zubida, H. (2012, July). Israel studies: An anthology: Patterns of immigration and absorption in Israel. *Jewish Virtual Library*. Retrieved from http://www. jewishvirtuallibrary.org/israel-studies-an-anthology-immigration-in-israel

2

Printed in Poland
by Amazon Fulfillment
Poland Sp. z o.o., Wrocław